YOUR TIME IS NOW
DEVOTIONAL

YOUR TIME IS NOW

DEVOTIONAL

**Daily Inspirations to Go Get
What God Has Given You**

JONATHAN EVANS

BETHANYHOUSE
a division of Baker Publishing Group
Minneapolis, Minnesota

Published by Bethany House Publishers
11400 Hampshire Avenue South
Minneapolis, Minnesota 55438
www.bethanyhouse.com

Bethany House Publishers is a division of
Baker Publishing Group, Grand Rapids, Michigan

Printed in the United States of America

Library of Congress Cataloging-in-Publication Data
Names: Evans, Jonathan, author.
Title: Your time is now devotional : daily inspirations to go get what God has
    given you / Jonathan Evans.
Description: Minneapolis, Minnesota : Bethany House Publishers, a division of
    Baker Publishing Group, [2022]
Identifiers: LCCN 2021043347 | ISBN 9780764238819 (paperback) | ISBN
    9780764240683 (casebound) | ISBN 9781493435777 (ebook)
Subjects: LCSH: Self-actualization (Psychology)—Religious aspects—
    Christianity—Prayers and devotions. | Christian life—Prayers and devotions. |
    Joshua (Biblical)—Prayers and devotions.
Classification: LCC BV4598.2 .E933 2022 | DDC 158.1—dc23
LC record available at https://lccn.loc.gov/2021043347

Cover design by Rob Williams, InsideOut Creative Arts, Inc.

Baker Publishing Group publications use paper produced from sustainable forestry practices and post-consumer waste whenever possible.

22 23 24 25 26 27 28   7 6 5 4 3 2 1

CONTENTS

Introduction   7

PART 1: Now   9

PART 2: But   31

PART 3: Look   57

PART 4: Go   77

PART 5: Dress   103

PART 6: Confidence   125

PART 7: Wait   155

PART 8: Yes   173

PART 9: Now   189

About the Author   206

INTRODUCTION

God has amazing plans for you—to give you hope and a future and to make you great in His work and His kingdom. Each of the following ninety devotions will help you grab hold of those plans *right now*.

Join us as we unpack what living fully in God's kingdom looks like and means for you. The inspirational truths about God's transforming power will encourage and equip you to engage victoriously with God, others, and yourself.

PART 1

THE *NOW* OF LIFE'S UNEXPECTED SWITCHES

> Trust in the LORD with all your heart and do not lean on your own understanding. In all your ways acknowledge Him, and He will make your paths straight.
>
> —PROVERBS 3:5-6

Football was my go-to, the thing I loved most. After months of weights, drills, practices, scrimmages, and games for what seemed like an endless cycle of years, I finally made it to the NFL. I was drafted to play for the Dallas Cowboys.

Now was my time! I had arrived, and I was ready for all God had in store.

Unfortunately, just two months after I was signed, the guy we all called "the grim reaper" stopped me one morning and informed me that I had been cut from the team. I had to gather my things and go. No more hanging around. No more rubbing shoulders with the greats. No more chances to prove myself. I had been released and needed to head out *now*.

Now . . .

The word can bring hope or pain. It can make us happy or sad. Our positive or negative *now* focus will determine how we respond, and one thing is for sure—we will react.

This *now* reality sets the stage for something new. No more planning, analyzing, or choosing. It's *go* time.

It's painful to experience being set aside, to be marginalized in an area where we felt competent and confident. But that isn't the end of our story. Maybe God is setting us free to pursue something even greater.

Application

1. Think about a time when you got cut from something important to you. How did you react?
2. Have you ever considered that your unexpected switch may be what God is using to place you in a better position? Why or why not?
3. In what ways can you prepare your mindset for the next *now* switch that comes your way?

Prayer

God, when anticipation fizzles, I don't always understand the why of the now, but I know You do. Help me trust that You will lead me in the right direction. Amen.

THE *NOW* OF FOLLOWING GOD WHEN HE MOVES

Now arise, cross this Jordan, you and all this people,
to the land which I am giving to them, to the sons of
Israel.

—JOSHUA 1:2

Joshua and the entire Israelite nation were in mourning. Their leader, Moses, had just died. Yet in the midst of their grief, God called them to continue onward under new leadership. It was Joshua's turn to lead *now*.

Now is a current word. It's about timing. No more procrastinating. No more waiting. No more messing around. When someone says now, they mean *now*.

God doesn't always wait until we feel ready to make His move. He doesn't always give us time to recover from life's bruises or knockdowns. He doesn't sit around until we give Him the green light. When God is ready to do something, He does it right then.

Much of the success or failure people experience is due to their ability, or inability, to respond when life changes as quickly as it did for Joshua. A person's capacity to adapt will determine their ability to achieve their goals and embrace the now moments in such a way that propels them forward rather than keeping them stuck in a routine or role they have held so long because they have gotten used to it.

If you want to move ahead into what God is ready for you to embrace and experience, then you need to be ready to say yes when He says *now*—even if the timing seems the worst. Because in God's timeframe, the worst of now is actually the best.

Application

1. Why does an inconvenient time become so difficult when God says to move now?
2. What determines whether we move forward?
3. What lesson can you take with you for the next challenge in your life?

Prayer

Father, Your timing is different from mine, I know. When You call me to move, even when it's inconvenient, give me the strength to say yes. Amen.

THE *NOW* OF STEPPING AWAY FROM ANOTHER'S COATTAILS

> Now it came about after the death of Moses the servant of the Lord, that the Lord spoke to Joshua the son of Nun, Moses' servant.
>
> —JOSHUA 1:1

Before Moses' death, Joshua had spent his whole career playing follower. He had put in his time, gotten the call, and made the cut. Now everything was about to change for Joshua. Now was his time to assume the mantle of leadership.

The word *now* informed Joshua that he could no longer ride the coattails of his mentor. He could no longer piggyback on Moses' leadership. It was time for him to step up and step out.

When God calls us, it's not okay to sit on the sidelines while other people take the field. This is the time when we can no longer ride the coattails of others. We still have a part to play even when the role, career field, or schedule is not what we had hoped for or planned.

But whether your life looks like you want it to or not, God has you there for a reason. This is your season. Your time is now to get what God has given you by fulfilling the plans He has for you to do. The question, though, is, Will you go get it?

Application

1. What may be holding you back from stepping into a leadership role that God may be calling you to? Why?
2. What might it look like for you to stop riding on someone else's coattails?
3. Which is more important, trust or preparation, in responding to God's call?

Prayer

God, when it's time for me to step forward into what You have planned, let me not feel so inadequate that I must rely on others to do what You've grown me to do. Amen.

THE *NOW* OF MAKING YOUR OWN RELATIONSHIP WITH GOD

As for me and my house, we will serve the LORD.
—JOSHUA 24:15

The spiritual life is a life of development. It has valleys, mountains, and wilderness seasons. Like sports, it has changes in the coaching staff, in the equipment personnel, or even on the roster itself. But as we grow and develop, we reach that point along the way when God is calling each of us to a whole new level of engagement with himself.

God may be calling us to step away into a different role. Part of stepping away means that we can't rely on someone else's relationship with God to carry us. Joshua had always relied on Moses' skills and accomplishments. After all, it had been Moses who received the Ten Commandments, who had talked to God as a friend, and who glowed from God's presence.

But now Joshua needed to step up and stand securely in his own relationship with God.

God is asking the same of us. We can no longer solely rely on the testimonies of our mentors, parents, or influencers. This new season means it's time for us to have our own testimonies. Our own stories. Our own victories. Our own illustrations. Our own ability to hear God's voice. It means no more procrastinating on passionately pursuing the thing that matters most—our connection to our Creator.

God wants a personal relationship with you. He wants you to rely on Him in learning your lessons and developing your skills.

Application

1. What makes stepping out on your own into something new so scary?
2. What are some things you need to know about God that would help you have a better relationship with Him?
3. How does a personal relationship with God connect you not only to God but also to other people?

Prayer

Father, help me to gain more understanding about You so my love and devotion to You become stronger. Amen.

THE *NOW* OF ENDING PROCRASTINATION

How long will you put off entering to take possession of the land which the LORD, the God of your fathers, has given you?

—JOSHUA 18:3

Our son J2 understands the word *now*. Before we started homeschooling our kids, each Monday after school he would come home and finish his entire week's homework packet. J2 wanted it all done so he could be free for the rest of the week to do what he wanted.

Our daughter Kelsey didn't care too much for the word *now*. She liked to procrastinate, especially on her schoolwork. She would do just about anything other than the work she had been given. Whenever my wife and I confronted her after her playtime, she whined and complained that she was too tired and miserable and didn't feel like it. But we insisted that she do her work before bedtime. Why? Because she wasn't being graded on her playing but on her schoolwork.

Many of us are procrastinating on our spiritual work while running ourselves ragged in the culture. We chase money, friends, fame, or fun. Too many of us choose to delay our spiritual assignments while instead spending all our energy focused on nonessential activities that are not even on God's grading scale for our lives. Procrastinating will get us nowhere but further behind. Instead, let's be like J2—working ahead and planning ahead so we can be better able and energized to move ahead.

Application

1. Do you identify more with J2 or Kelsey? How so?
2. What past experiences have molded you to either forge ahead or put things off?
3. What consequences of procrastination can you identify that might help you stay focused?

Prayer

Father, help me to better understand my strengths and weaknesses so I can organize my priorities and serve You and others more faithfully. Give me the energy and drive to not put off until later what I need to do now. Amen.

THE *NOW* OF LAYING YOUR PURPOSE'S FOUNDATION

Delight yourself in the Lord; and He will give you the desires of your heart.

—PSALM 37:4

My daughter Kelsey isn't fond of doing homework. She knows it's important in the long run, but in the short term, she'd prefer to focus her energies on other things—things less difficult and more fun. Her motto is "I'll work on that later." And she'd be perfectly happy if later never came.

The problem with that thinking, of course, is that her focus is too narrow. She has her fun time wrestling with her brothers or bouncing on a trampoline. She hasn't discovered the joy that is in learning and accomplishing things from work.

The same is true for us in our spiritual lives. If we want to pursue God's best for us, we need to stand on a solid faith foundation. When we stand before God, we aren't going to get graded on how we played the secular game of life. When we stand before God, we aren't even going to get graded on the things we ran ourselves ragged pursuing for fun. When we stand before God, we will be graded on one thing and one thing only: our spiritual work. God will be evaluating not only what we did but our attitude while doing it.

Serving God is not just a duty. It can come with much delight and joy. Now is our time. Now is our season.

Application

1. What is keeping you from living out the full expression of your reason for being on this earth?
2. What do you need to set aside to have a vacancy for God to step into?
3. Is it possible to reevaluate your work efforts so you can find joy and delight in them instead of viewing them as obligations?

Prayer

Father, help me to take delight in all that I do in serving You so I can experience Your kind of joy. Amen.

THE *NOW* OF ALLOWING SOMETHING SIGNIFICANT TO DIE

> Moses the servant of the LORD died there in the land of Moab, in accordance with the word of the LORD.
> —DEUTERONOMY 34:5

As long as Moses was living, Joshua was listening to Moses and not to God. But after Moses died, Joshua stepped into his purpose and heard from God himself.

Too many of us have become content watching everyone else pursue their passions and live out their purposes. We say we want to pursue our own, but we feel it's safer to stay behind the screen and just watch others. We've become too afraid to try. Or too wounded from past pain. Too timid. Too cynical. Too stuck.

God knows this. That's why sometimes, as in the case of Joshua, we recognize that something significant has to die in our lives for us to come to an awareness that it's time to move. It was only after the death of Moses that Joshua was able to hear from God.

Some things, such as addictions and bad behaviors, are counterproductive and we need to overcome them. But sometimes even good things can have adverse consequences. It wasn't until Joshua let Moses go that he was able to live out the fullness of all he had been gifted to do.

Whenever we are going through a season where we have lost something or someone we counted on, we must keep our eyes open through the tears. Our loss might be a person, occupation, health status, relationship, or ministry. That is often the very time when God can get our authentic attention.

Application

1. What in your life has to die in order for you to hear God's voice?
2. Do you have anything that needs to be laid to rest in order for you to experience God's presence and guidance?
3. What discoveries and choices can you make that will help you find a place of service?

Prayer

Lord, help me turn my losses into gains so I can see Your hand on my life as I serve You. Amen.

THE *NOW* OF GETTING UNSTUCK FROM GOOD THINGS

After that He went out and looked at a tax collector named Levi sitting in the tax office, and He said to him, "Follow Me." And he left everything behind, and got up and began following Him.

—LUKE 5:27-28

It is frequently the good things in life that keep us dependent. If we are not careful, the good things can keep us stuck. They can keep us bound to what is *good* and unable to pursue what is *best*. God knows that for each of us to live out what He has called us to do, we need to be dependent on only one Source, which is Him. We must reassess our need for notoriety, financial success, personal approval, family acceptance, or cultural clout. Which is why a lot of times God will take those things from us. But sometimes He will ask *us* to remove them. He does this so we will have no choice but to have a vacancy in our lives where He can step in.

We may have some great things in our lives, or even great people, that can't go where we are going. We may have to tell them, "Hey, I love you, but I just can't take you with me." We may have to step away from some situations, relationships, or even opportunities in order to step into God's plan for our lives. But doesn't God have our best interests at heart? And isn't this what learning to trust Him is all about?

Application

1. Do you have good things in your life that may be keeping you from the *best* things?
2. What blessing do you have that may actually be taking you further away from the Blesser?
3. Is there something, or someone, stopping you from hearing the voice of God? What steps can you take to change that?

Prayer

God, give me eyes to see what is really important as I fulfill Your calling on my life. Amen.

THE *NOW* OF DITCHING IDOLS

You shall have no other gods before Me.
—EXODUS 20:3

I've known athletes who live and breathe sports. If a game is scheduled, then *nothing* can get in their way—not friends, not family, not even God. If they're out to eat with their family, and a television on the wall is showing a sporting event, their focus goes—and remains—in that direction. They would do *anything* for sports. The Bible calls this an idol. An idol is anything that superimposes its own importance over God's. Whenever we have something or someone taking God's position in our lives, it blocks God from speaking to us.

We all have seen firsthand how things like sports can become so important they become idols. It's almost like a religious devotion that gets in the way of family, friends, work, and life itself.

The problem is that these idols get in the way of our relationships with family and especially with God. We can make idols out of just about anything. Work, money, success, social media likes, and even church can become idols. We can get so caught up in the performance of worship leaders. Or we might show so much reverence and adoration for the church building that we forget it's God and His people we should be giving devotion and love to.

It's not that we must abandon sports or gathering for worship. It's just that we must see that these things do not come before God.

Application

1. How would you describe the attitudes and actions of those who make sports their religion?
2. How is it that we can make the church building and aspects of worship more important than God?
3. What needs do you have that can either help or hinder you from prioritizing God in your daily life?

Prayer

God, give me the wisdom to order my priorities so that You are always first in my thoughts and affections. Amen.

THE *NOW* OF BEING TOO COMFORTABLE

A wide door for effective service has opened to me, and there are many adversaries.

—1 CORINTHIANS 16:9

When I was let go from the Dallas Cowboys, I wound up watching the entire football season from home on my couch. Had I become comfortable sitting on the couch while watching everyone else play football, I wouldn't be where I am today.

I knew if I was going to have any shot at something more than simply staring at a television screen, I would have to learn how to hear from God on what to do *now*. When we fixate on what we've lost, we forget that God has great plans for each of us to live out (Jeremiah 29:11). Or we become comfortable just staying where we are. It's easy, causes less hassle, and offers less risk. But it also provides less reward.

God is calling us to go further, rise higher, and achieve more in His name than we can imagine. But we will never experience all that God has for us unless we are willing to rise up out of the depths of our own disappointments, get up off the couch of our own comfort zone, and pursue His plan for this season. *Now*. Not tomorrow. Not next year. Not when our emotions have had a chance to heal or we've had an opportunity to try everything else out first. Not even when we feel more prepared and ready. No, our time is *now*. It's up to us to get up and go get what God has given us.

Application

1. What makes you get discouraged easily?
2. What are the adversaries that might be keeping you on the couch?
3. In what ways can you more intentionally look for God's open door?

Prayer

God, give me the strength and courage to adventure off my couch and through my new door of opportunity. Amen.

PART 2

THE *BUT* OF DISOBEDIENCE

But the sons of Israel acted unfaithfully regarding the things designated for destruction . . . therefore the anger of the Lord burned against the sons of Israel.

—JOSHUA 7:1

After directing millions of people across a raging river during flood season, Joshua got them to shout and march around the walls of the well-defended city of Jericho. Doing so brought those massive walls crashing down.

Joshua had his own style and strategies. He led differently from his predecessor, Moses. Everyone saw that. They also saw that his approach was working. The Israelites were winning.

But.

Even though Joshua and his warriors were whipping through their battles like wild men, things quickly went south. God had commanded the people of Israel to destroy everything once they'd conquered a place, *but* one man named Achan took what was supposed to be destroyed. As a result, not only did everything turn on a dime for him, but it changed for everyone else as well. In an instant.

Up until that point, the Israelites had been feared, *but*.

In just one short syllable the entire trajectory of a statement got turned around, reversed.

But the sons of Israel acted unfaithfully, and their winning streak halted. Just like that. The victories they had come to expect were no longer within their grasp. All because of a man who had a change of heart.

If we want to enjoy the blessings God has in store for us, then we need to be diligent about heeding His commands and safeguarding our hearts. Only then can we stay away from the dangerous *but*.

Application

1. In what ways have you seen a *but* reverse your course? What happened as a result?
2. Have any pursuits or possessions wooed you away from obeying God?
3. What are some steps you can take to ensure you don't have a change of heart?

Prayer

God, I commit to faithfully obeying your commands. Strengthen my determination and my heart. Amen.

THE *BUT* OF PRIDE

> Pride goes before destruction, and a haughty spirit before stumbling.
>
> —PROVERBS 16:18

Achan had a problem—and it started before he took items that God had banned.

God had been with the Israelites through all of their battles and victories. They had ridden the high road to fame and success. I imagine you know what success can do to a person as much as I do. It can cause someone to start reading their own reviews, believing their own press, getting a big head. Which is exactly what happened to Achan—*and* to other Israelites.

Even though Achan was singled out, he wasn't the only one involved. As Joshua 7:1 tells us, "But the sons of Israel acted unfaithfully." No doubt Achan had help carrying his load of loot.

The Israelites had gone from riding the winds of God's favor to suffering the scourge of His anger. All because in the midst of their success, they caved in to pride and selfishness. Vanity led to Achan's decision to take what wasn't his. And vanity led to destruction.

When life starts going well for us and we're on a roll, it's important that we don't get too big for our britches

34

and think God's rules no longer apply to us. We act on our pride, and we surely set ourselves up to stumble.

Application

1. What prideful attitudes do you need to confront and confess?
2. In what ways have you seen others stumble because of a haughty spirit?
3. What steps can you take to keep a close check on your attitude and mindset?

Prayer

Father, sometimes I think of myself more highly than I should. I know that doesn't please You and gets in the way of my being able to hear and follow You as I should. Replace my pride with humility so I will always honor and obey You. Amen.

THE *BUT* OF OVERSTEPPING BOUNDARIES

> The LORD God commanded the man, saying, "From any tree of the garden you may freely eat; but from the tree of the knowledge of good and evil you shall not eat, for on the day that you eat from it you will certainly die."
>
> —GENESIS 2:16–17

Adam and Eve had only one boundary in the garden of Eden: to stay away from the Tree of the Knowledge of Good and Evil. Not a big deal, since they had everything else. They lived in a perfect place, had a perfect relationship, had all their needs perfectly supplied. Yet they focused on the one tree marked "off-limits."

When Adam and Eve overstepped the boundaries God had given them, they paid the price. They went from enjoying freedom, provision, and victory . . . *but*.

Adam and Eve had a perfect marriage in a perfect environment, *but* now they had dissension in their relationship. Adam and Eve had easy access to an abundance of food, *but* now Adam had to toil in sweat to cultivate the ground.

But they got kicked out of the garden. *But* Eve had pain in childbirth. *But* their son Cain killed their son Abel. *But, but, but*.

They knowingly overstepped a boundary and changed perfection to brokenness with one simple act. How often we do the same thing. God gives us good limits that provide freedom, provision, and victory, *but* we rebel.

The next time we find ourselves unsatisfied with what God has provided, we can let Adam and Eve be our warning alarm—that though something off-limits seems okay, it can bring unwanted change in a hurry.

Application

1. Think about a boundary you crossed. What was it? Why did you cross it? What was the result?
2. Why might it be easy to rationalize your decision to rebel against God's healthy boundaries?
3. How does knowing God's will affect your commitment to boundaries and freedom?

Prayer

God, give me the wisdom and strength to walk within Your boundaries by keeping my focus on the freedoms You have already given me. Amen.

THE *BUT* OF TAKING WHAT BELONGS TO OTHERS

> You shall not covet your neighbor's house; you shall not covet your neighbor's wife, or his male slave, or his female slave, or his ox, or his donkey, or anything that belongs to your neighbor.
>
> —EXODUS 20:17

King David saw beautiful Bathsheba, a married woman, and took her. But the moment he did, he lost everything. God had already given David victory after victory. He had already made him first in line when he had once been last in line (see 1 Samuel 16). God had already given him victory over Goliath. He had given him victory when escaping King Saul, who tried to keep him from becoming the next king. David had overcome everything he faced.

But now David sat one morning with only one thing on his mind, and he chose not to control himself from pursuing it. He couldn't stay in the stewardship mindset of gratefully receiving God's blessings, so he chose to take someone else's wife.

If someone had only told David that doing so would have disastrous results, maybe he would have stopped before he started. *But* because of his decision, he would soon lose a child and would wind up with one of his sons killing another of his sons. But he went after what wasn't his and wound up with family anarchy on his hands. His own son would later seek to kill him for the throne.

He wanted to take what he had and add to it to go further than God said he could go.

David's story is an important lesson for us: Whenever we take what belongs to others, we transform our greatest victories into our greatest defeats.

Application

1. What might you be taking that belongs to others? A relationship? An item? Recognition? Why?

2. In what ways can you prevent yourself from coveting something or someone that doesn't belong to you?

3. When has wanting something taken you by surprise? How will you be ready for it next time?

Prayer

Father, You have given me more blessings than I can even count. Forgive me for trying to add to them by taking what doesn't belong to me. Amen.

THE *BUT* OF WITHHOLDING FROM GOD

But a man named Ananias, with his wife Sapphira, sold a piece of property, and kept back some of the proceeds for himself, with his wife's full knowledge, and bringing a portion of it, he laid it at the apostles' feet.

—ACTS 5:1-2

Ananias and Sapphira were a wealthy, respected couple in the early church who sold their land for a great price. They gave some proceeds to the church's work, but they kept some of the profit for themselves and then lied about it. As a result of wanting more, they got less—both of them died.

Though that's an extreme example, it shows how serious God is about integrity and generosity. He can do so much more with and in our lives than we can on our own. His blessings are always much better than what we get when we try to hoard rather than freely give. The truth is that when we withhold from God, something really does die within us—the victories and freedom God has planned for us. Withholding isn't worth losing a part of ourselves. Give freely to God and receive a different and more valuable treasure that He has waiting for you.

Application

1. In what ways are you seeking to act like an owner rather than a manager of what God's given to you?
2. Do you struggle to give yourself and your possessions completely to God? Why or why not?
3. What steps can you take to make yourself more available to freely give everything you are and have to God?

Prayer

Father, I don't want to withhold who I am or what I have—it's all Yours anyway. Strengthen my eyes, my hands, and my heart to remember that I am stewarding and managing everything for Your glory. Amen.

THE *BUT* OF TAKING WHAT BELONGS TO GOD

> Would anyone rob God? Yet you are robbing Me! But you say, "How have we robbed You?" In tithes and offerings.
>
> —MALACHI 3:8

In the days of Malachi, things seemed to be going well. But when religious leaders and common people alike came to worship God, they showed disrespect and contempt for Him by bringing blind, injured, and sick animals as sacrifices. They often preached one thing but practiced another. They focused on their own needs rather than their relationship with God.

It's easy when we are experiencing victories in our businesses, or our talents, or our relationships to think we accomplished them by ourselves. It's easy just to help ourselves to the extra spoils of success rather than remember that everything belongs to God.

But . . . that's why Malachi 3:8 says that we rob God when we don't remember Him and offer our best to Him. We can only rob God of something that isn't ours to begin with. When we selfishly keep the plunders of our victory, God places a *but* in our paths. We've been caught.

And yet, when we choose to remember Him in gratitude, this is what He promises: "'Bring the whole tithe into the storehouse, so that there may be food in My house, and put Me to the test now in this,' says the LORD of armies, 'if I do not open for you the windows of heaven and pour out for you a blessing until it overflows'" (Malachi 3:10).

I like that kind of response when we gratefully give back to Him what He already owns, don't you?

Application

1. Do you regularly give back to God what is His through tithing? If not, what's holding you back?
2. How does it change the conversation to realize that everything you have belongs to God anyway?
3. In what ways have you experienced God's blessing as He speaks of it in Malachi 3:10?

Prayer

God, as I give back to You what You already own, help me to remember that my blessings and victories exist because of You. Amen.

THE *BUT* OF RECREATING GOD'S DESIGN IN MARRIAGE

Marriage is to be held in honor among all.
—HEBREWS 13:4

One of the greatest victories we can have is an honoring and respectful marriage. The apostle Paul gave us the recipe for that kind of marriage when he wrote that we must "submit to one another out of reverence for Christ" (Ephesians 5:21 NIV). Wives do this by submitting to and respecting their husbands, and husbands do this by loving their wives so much they would die for them. This is a recipe for peace and joy.

But . . . we run into disaster when we don't want to follow that recipe. Instead, we want to change our marriage to fit our own perspectives. We fight for control and to have our own expectations fulfilled. Then we wonder what has happened when conflict continually shows up in our homes. It's because we have taken our own ideas and implanted them into the victory of the marriage God has given us, turning it into a swift defeat.

Let's step back and let go of our attempts to recreate God's design for marriage. Let's open ourselves up to the possibility of serving our spouses. And watch the victories come.

Application

1. If you're married, what can you do to show your spouse that you accept and love them as a person created in God's image? If you aren't married but you want to be, how can you prepare to keep your commitment as a future mate?
2. In what ways can unmet needs and unfulfilled expectations bring conflict into marriage?
3. What might be some expectations and perspectives that you need to get rid of to see your spouse in a new light?

Prayer

God, help me see my marriage as good and my spouse as a gift from You. When I'm tempted to give in to feelings of unfulfilled expectations, remind me that this person is part of Your plan to grow me into victory and maturity. Amen.

THE *BUT* OF RAISING KIDS IN OUR OWN IMAGE

Fathers, do not provoke your children to anger, but bring them up in the discipline and instruction of the Lord.

—EPHESIANS 6:4

I've got five children, so I'm constantly learning, constantly studying, constantly seeking God's ways for me to lead my family. One thing has stood out from the start, and that is the reality that God has entrusted my children to me and my wife, Kanika, to raise, but they belong to Him. As God said, "Let Us make mankind in Our image, according to Our likeness" (Genesis 1:26).

Our children are His. God didn't bless Kanika and me with children so we can have look-alikes. He did it so *He* will have look-alikes. It's our role to raise them to resemble Him. This is about God, not us.

We are training up our children to become like Christ. Our choices, attitudes, and actions shape their little lives and affect their destinies. The best thing we can hear someone tell us isn't, "Oh, your kids look and act just like you!" Rather, it's, "Oh, your kids look and act just like Jesus!"

That means we need to understand how we became Christians and what steps we took and concepts we gathered that helped us to become like Jesus. After all, we can only teach what we already know.

Application

1. Does your parenting leadership bring glory to you or to God?

2. In whose image are you forming your children? Yours or God's?

3. Are you living a life of faith in front of your children, or just talking about it? In what ways can you actively mentor your children in the things of God?

Prayer

Father, thank You that You've entrusted these children to me so I can raise them to become like Christ. Help me not to forget that they are Yours so that I don't try to create them in my image, because I know that will bring a but *of disaster into their lives. Instead, let my focus be on preparing them for the destiny You have in store for them. Amen.*

THE *BUT* OF TWISTING GOD'S TRUTHS

I walk in the way of righteousness, in the midst of the paths of justice.

—PROVERBS 8:20

Multiple times the Bible says the anger of the Lord burned against the sons of Israel because of what their nation did. Any time we take what isn't ours, we open ourselves up to God's wrath. Our nation has been taking and twisting the truths of God into its own version of reality in many ways, and then we wonder why chaos ensues all over our land. One of the issues we've twisted is justice. Our culture has taken the definition of justice and displaced it. We've marginalized it. We've stuck it on a dusty shelf out of sight as we've skipped over Psalm 89:14, which says, "Righteousness and justice are the foundation of Your throne; mercy and truth go before You."

Both righteousness and justice are the foundations of God's kingdom. What happens when we take half of a foundation out from under anything? Consider taking half a foundation out from underneath a skyscraper. What if you took half the foundation out from under the launch pad at the Kennedy Space Center? Or what if you removed half of the foundation from under your own house?

You get the point. Removing half of a foundation from anything will lead to its sudden destruction. Justice and righteousness go hand in hand. We must pursue both so we can experience God's blessing instead of His wrath.

Application

1. Is there a wrong that you need to make right?
2. What steps can you take to begin that process?
3. What justice can you pursue for someone in your area of influence today as you follow Jesus?

Prayer

Lord, as I practice righteousness and justice in my life, give me Your wisdom to make sure I'm on a full foundation and not trying to build Your kingdom on just half a foundation. Amen.

THE *BUT* OF STANDING AGAINST YOUR ENEMIES

> You cannot stand against your enemies until you have removed the designated things from your midst.
>
> —JOSHUA 7:13

The Dallas Cowboys are one of the greatest NFL teams. They've won five Super Bowls and have had legendary players—Troy Aikman, Emmitt Smith, Michael Irvin, Nate Newton, Darren Woodson. But as legendary as they may be, the trophies they won belong to the Cowboys organization and not the players.

If any one of them were to decide, "I'm going to take that trophy home now," he would soon go from champion to convict.

In Joshua 7, we learn that because of Achan's sin, the Israelites got beat big-time in the battle at Ai. The Israelites' defeat was so drastic that everyone reeled in its wake. When Joshua asked God why He had brought them out there only to humiliate them at the hands of their enemies, God gave an insightful and quick reply: Israel had sinned by taking banned items. Because of that, they would no longer be able to stand against their enemies until they made things right.

Think about your own wins and losses. Perhaps a dependence on people's approval, an ambition beyond His plans, or even a hunger for pleasure will prevent you from a healthy commitment toward personal growth and kingdom impact. Whatever it is, you're better off without it. Walk away from it so you can rise to win again.

Application

1. Do you have anything in your life, whether good or bad, that God may want you to put down so you can get back on track?

2. In what ways have you seen a connection between walking with God and standing up against the things or people who try to hold you back?

3. Have you ever considered that your wrong actions negatively affect others in ways you may not even realize?

Prayer

God, You are more important than anything or anyone. Help me let go of those things that keep me distracted from Your plans for me. Amen.

THE *BUT* OF MOVING AHEAD OF GOD

Wait for the LORD; be strong and let your heart take courage; yes, wait for the LORD.

—PSALM 27:14

When Achan chose to cross God's boundary, he paid a steep price: death. The sad thing is that if he had just waited a bit longer, he would have gotten even more of what God planned to give him. Case in point, in the second battle against Ai, God told Joshua that the spoils were theirs to keep. Joshua 8:2 records God's plan: "You shall do to Ai and its king just as you did to Jericho and its king; you shall take only its spoil and its cattle as plunder for yourselves."

Think about that. The first battle: no treasure. The second battle: abundant treasure.

Had Achan obeyed and waited, he would have gotten a rich reward! But he didn't make it that far. God had the spoils planned for him to have all the time, but Achan wasn't there to receive them when it was the right time to get them. Achan missed out on all God had planned to give to him because he jumped the gun in his greed and gave to himself.

Sometimes we get impatient because we want to see the rewards and victories *now*! So we take matters into our own hands—*but* it isn't God's timing yet. God knows the bigger picture. When He tells us to wait, it isn't to punish us or to be cruel but to ensure that we are ready to experience and accept the blessings and victories.

Application

1. When have you been tempted to push ahead with your own plans rather than wait on God? What was the result?
2. What do you think God wants you to do during the waiting period?
3. When have you waited on God? What was the result?

Prayer

Father, forgive me for the times when I've rushed ahead of You. Plant wisdom within me so I can see the power of waiting and then follow through for the blessings. Amen.

THE *BUT* OF GETTING IN YOUR OWN WAY

> Do you not know that those who run in a race all run, but only one receives the prize? Run in such a way that you may win.
>
> —1 CORINTHIANS 9:24

During the COVID-19 pandemic in 2020 I couldn't be at any NFL games. As the Cowboys' chaplain, I still wanted to be there for them to process what they were going through in this monumental shift of not allowing fans in the stadiums.

At first the players didn't know how they would play at full capacity when all the energy that once surrounded and motivated them was gone. After a few games, however, the players realized that the loss of the fans around them actually forced them to focus on their internal competence.

In fact, once they started playing and focusing on the game plan and plays called from the head coach, they realized that they didn't need to be dependent on what was going on outside of them. They had what they needed to win—their shoulder pads, their helmets, their playbook, their calls, their skill sets.

It isn't always the devil who defeats us Christians. Too often, the root cause is our own choices. Our own impulsive greed. Sometimes it's *us* giving up the offensive. It's us giving up God's favor, His victory, and His hand in our lives.

But. You can stop that cycle right now. If you will just decide to let go of the external influences and focus on the internal relationship with the Spirit and His rule over your heart and your mind instead, you'll move forward. You'll advance. You'll win.

Application

1. What external forces do you rely on too much for your success?
2. How can you switch from competing with others to focusing on your own best efforts?
3. What are some ways you can focus on the internal relationship with the Holy Spirit to move you forward in life?

Prayer

God, when I become tempted to rely on anything other than You, refocus my thoughts and energy back to You. Amen.

PART 3

LOOK

LOOK AWAY FROM THE DISTRACTIONS

Suddenly they looked around and saw no one with them anymore, except Jesus alone.

—MARK 9:8

Only Peter, James, and John were on the mount when Jesus was transfigured before them. These disciples got a glimpse into the spiritual realm. Not only did they see Jesus in brightly shining garments, but they also saw Moses and Elijah talking with Him. They had never had an experience like this before. They were quickly caught up in what they were seeing. The Bible tells us, "A cloud formed, overshadowing them, and a voice came out of the cloud: 'This is My beloved Son; listen to Him!'" (Mark 9:7). Then everything from this spiritual display disappeared and all they saw was Jesus.

Imagine being there with those disciples. The event was to help them get a better view of Jesus, but they became distracted by the other sights. We get this way sometimes during both personal devotions and corporate worship.

Distractions show that we haven't trained ourselves to figure out what is most important at any given moment in our lives and relationships. Where we look matters a lot. Look away from the road at some distraction while driving, and the car will begin to drift out of its lane. If a quarterback looks left while throwing right, the whole defense, including the quarterback himself, can miss the play. Distractions can be detrimental.

Application

1. What things have distracted you while in conversation with someone? How did the other person react? How did you react when someone else was distracted while you were talking?
2. What things have distracted you in your private and public times of worship?
3. Why do you think we get so distracted so easily?

Prayer

Father, help me understand what is most important at the moment so I can center my full attention there. Amen.

LOOK TOWARD GOING OUT ON TOP

> If it is disagreeable in your sight to serve the Lord, choose for yourselves today whom you will serve: whether the gods which your fathers served which were beyond the River, or the gods of the Amorites in whose land you are living; but as for me and my house, we will serve the Lord.
>
> —JOSHUA 24:15 NASB1995

Where God looks matters. When it came to Joshua, the Israelites, and the battles at Ai, God wanted to see whether the hearts of the Israelites were surrendered to Him. He didn't look at their muscle, their formation, or their skills. When He saw that Achan's heart was not where it needed to be, He allowed the Israelites to lose the entire battle.

Joshua and his men didn't just sit down and lick their wounds after their first loss. They got back up, made sure everyone's heart was right with God, and took Ai by force. Joshua rounded up thirty thousand of his best men and stormed the city and set it on fire.

Joshua meant those words about serving God. He led many more victories for the Israelites as they conquered their land of promise. His household served God because he served God. Even those who came after Joshua served God simply because his legacy was locked in.

He had done things right, and he went out on top.

Application

1. What religious person do you know personally who fell flat in spiritual defeat because they didn't live what they had preached to others?
2. Do you ever experience times when you find it difficult to stay faithful in serving God? Why?
3. What can you do to establish your own legacy of faithfully serving God?

Prayer

Father, Your concern is about the condition of my heart. So help me to always keep it right with You. Amen.

LOOK FOR A LEADER
TO FOLLOW

You will guide me with Your plan, and afterward
receive me to glory.

—PSALM 73:24

Some think it's easy to look like a leader when we are
mentored by one. Why *wouldn't* Joshua succeed when
Moses had tutored him? It's like expecting a coach who
learned under a winning coach to win as well. We expect
him to know how to plan, prioritize, and make decisions.

I am leading others spiritually right now because Tony
Evans is my dad. I learned under the leadership of a father
with a doctorate in theology, an author of more than a
hundred books, and the first African American to write
a study Bible and full Bible commentary.

But what about those who don't have Moses as a mentor or Tony Evans as a father? What about those who come
from broken homes or grew up in foster care? Is there any
hope of living in such a way that we have a positive effect
on the lives of others?

It is good to lead others relationally, educationally, and
socially. But our best leadership comes when we model
learning spiritually from others. Jesus becomes our best
example, teacher, and guide. That is why He calls us to

follow Him. We have the example of how He related to others, the content of His teaching as we read the Bible, and the experience of His love, guidance, and faithfulness in our own lives. Following Jesus is what can make us not only look like a leader but become one.

Application

1. How do you understand and define success, especially in others?
2. Is success dependent on what you learn from others or on what you learn from your efforts?
3. In what ways can you follow the spiritual leadership of others to build your own spiritual leadership?

Prayer

Father, thank You for letting me follow You. Thank You for giving Jesus as a leader I can follow. Please help me to live faithfully so that others may see the quality of my example and give glory to You. Amen.

LOOK LIKE A LEADER

God does not see as man sees, since man looks at the
outward appearance, but the Lord looks at the heart.

—1 SAMUEL 16:7

Saul, the first king of Israel, sinned by disobeying God.
So God rejected him and sent Samuel to anoint one of
the eight sons of Jesse. Jesse brought seven of his sons
before Samuel. As Samuel met each son, he thought for
sure that this would be the one. But God rejected each
of them. Then Samuel asked if Jesse had any other sons.
He indicated that his youngest son was tending sheep. So
Samuel summoned him. When young David arrived, God
told Samuel that this was the one to anoint.

Jesse assumed that one of the seven oldest sons would
be the one. He did not bring David at first. Why? Psalm
51:5 suggests that David might have been an illegitimate
son and thus not qualified to become Israel's king. But
God chose David for what was in David's heart rather
than his physical appearance or heritage.

Everyone who follows Jesus comes with baggage.
Sometimes it's obvious to others. Sometimes only we are
fully aware of our faults, failures, and emotional scars.

God will often go to the back of the line to bring someone to the front. He goes to those who appear unlikely.
He goes to those who were never even invited to the table.

God chooses how and whom He calls. In spite of what you may have done or may be thinking, the God we serve supersedes it all. He gets to choose. And He's chosen you.

Application

1. What are some of the excuses or reasons you have for not wanting to lead others?
2. What emotional scars and baggage may be holding you back from serving God?
3. How can you ensure that your heart is right with God so you can effectively follow and serve Him?

Prayer

Father, help me find healing for my emotional hang-ups and relational baggage so others can see You in my living and serving. Amen.

LOOK THE WAY GOD SEES

LORD, my heart is not proud, nor my eyes arrogant;
nor do I involve myself in great matters, or in things
too difficult for me.

—PSALM 131:1

Jesus told a parable of two men who entered the temple to pray. One was a spiritual leader, a Pharisee, and the other was a hated tax collector. While the Pharisee prayed, he said, "God, I thank You that I am not like other people: swindlers, crooked, adulterers, or even like this tax collector" (Luke 18:11). Then the Pharisee began to recite all the things he did for God that he thought made him a good person. Meanwhile, the tax collector wouldn't even raise his eyes toward heaven, but instead beat his chest in remorse and begged God to be merciful to him, a sinner. Jesus ended the parable by saying that the tax collector was the one God accepted.

What qualified the tax collector as opposed to the Pharisee? What was the thing that made him stand out to God? It was his heart.

God sees people differently and calls us to do the same. God had to remind His prophet Samuel that mankind sees the outer appearance but God looks at what is within. Stature doesn't hold a candle to a soul on fire for God.

The Pharisee may have looked the part. But the qualification for worldly acceptance is different from the qualification for God's kingdom influencers. That qualification rests solely on whether you have the right heart.

Application

1. What do you have to do to get your heart right with God?
2. How do you know when your heart is right with God?
3. How can you convey to others by your words or actions that your heart is right with God?

Prayer

Father, help me to always keep my heart centered on my relationship with You so that others may see You in the way I live and the way I relate to You and those around me. Amen.

LOOKING FOR APPROVAL

> David said, "The LORD who saved me from the paw of the lion and the paw of the bear, He will save me from the hand of this Philistine." So Saul said to David, "Go, and may the LORD be with you."
>
> —1 SAMUEL 17:37

David spent much of his youth caring for his father's flock of sheep. Evidently, David must have spent a lot of quiet time communing with God. He also became a good marksman with his slingshot. He must have learned to trust God for guidance and protection, since he was able to use this tool to kill both a lion and a bear that had attacked the flock.

Now Israel was being threatened by the Philistines, especially one giant of a man named Goliath. Since no one else would meet this challenge, David volunteered. He trusted God to give him success. And God guided the stone in David's slingshot that killed this giant and won the day for Israel. While the people approved of his victory, David was more concerned about keeping God's approval on his life.

It's become an obsession in our culture to seek people's approval and acceptance in what we say and post. But what's the point in amassing a huge number of followers if, at the same time, we are being scrolled past by God?

Your goal shouldn't be just to make it to the line inside the house when Samuel comes knocking. Your goal should be to have God on your side when you are confronted with giant-sized challenges.

Application

1. What are the personal issues you face in your times of challenge and trouble?
2. To whom do you look for inspiration, encouragement, and approval? Why?
3. What specifically are you doing to keep your faith and trust in God strong?

Prayer

Lord, help me keep my faith pure and strong in Your will and ways so that I may keep Your approval upon my life and service. Amen.

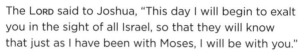

LOOK AND CHECK THE CONNECTION

> The LORD said to Joshua, "This day I will begin to exalt you in the sight of all Israel, so that they will know that just as I have been with Moses, I will be with you."
>
> —JOSHUA 3:7

When the iPhone first came out, my wife and I made our big purchase. We couldn't wait to get home, plug them in, and turn them on. When I plugged in my phone, it quickly made the *bing* sound and lit up. But Kanika's phone just stayed blank.

Here I was excited to finally explore my phone, but Kanika's face told me I needed to help her, and help her now. I could see the cord connected to the wall. Even so, I went over to the outlet and gave it a little extra push. Sure enough, *bing*. Nothing was wrong with the phone. It just didn't work because the plug hadn't made it all the way into the source.

Lots of people look and talk and act as if they are close to God. But when we look closely at the screen of their souls, nothing's there. It's blank. That's because they have not truly connected with the Source. You may be in the vicinity of the outlet, but being only partway plugged in doesn't work for your phone or your relationship with God.

Application

1. Is God more concerned with how you look or how you live?
2. What might be keeping you from connecting fully with God's life and love?
3. In what area or areas do you need to push forward to experience a real and life-changing connection with God? Is there anything you need to understand more clearly or to embrace more strongly to experience that life-changing connection with God?

Prayer

Lord, help me press forward until I am fully connected with You. Amen.

LOOK AT AND FACE YOUR FEARS

I sought the Lord and He answered me, and rescued me from all my fears.

—PSALM 34:4

Having five young kids means I get to see all the new children's movies. I especially liked *The Lion King*. The young lion, Simba, is trained by his father. But when Simba goes to a place he isn't supposed to go, his dad has to come and save him. And in the process, his dad dies.

Then his uncle Scar lies to Simba, blames him, and makes him feel fearful, depressed, and unworthy. All of these emotions cause Simba to run away. He questions his own abilities and starts hanging around others who are content to simply wander.

Then one day his father appears in a cloud to remind Simba that he is a king, destined to rule and guide others to safety. Simba musters up the courage to confront the lies of Scar and the pain of the past. He chooses to conquer them rather than be bound by them. As a result, he claims his calling on Pride Rock, leading those he was created to lead.

Our Savior died and redeemed us. He affirms that we can overcome the scars and situations of life that degrade us. God has called us to the top of the mountain in order to love and lead according to His principles and purposes.

You may be holding back from grasping who you really are in Christ because of fears or your past. But God has redeemed you, and He's already called you. He's waiting for you to take your rightful place by facing your scars and leaving them behind. They can only hold you back if you let them.

Application

1. What scars or fears have been holding you back from giving every part of your life to God?
2. What do you see that God has called you to do?
3. What would it take to embrace God's freedom from your fears?

Prayer

Father, strengthen my resolve to follow as You deliver me from my fears. Amen.

LOOK AT THE MIRROR'S REFLECTION

> We all, with unveiled faces, looking as in a mirror at the glory of the Lord, are being transformed into the same image from glory to glory, just as from the Lord, the Spirit.
>
> —2 CORINTHIANS 3:18

People find gold in nature mixed together with other minerals and impurities. To extract the gold, they must heat it over a hot fire. The gold sinks to the bottom of the container while the impurities float to the top. The refiner neither knows nor cares about what the impurities are. He is only interested in the gold. So he repeatedly skims off the impurities until only pure gold remains. When does this process end? When he can see his own reflection in the molten gold.

God sees something of value in each of us. It's like spiritual gold. But we have lots of impurities that must be removed. Paul gives us this promise: "Just as we have borne the image of the earthy, we will also bear the image of the heavenly" (1 Corinthians 15:49). That's why we face tests, trials, troubles, difficulties, and lots of challenges.

God uses our adversities to remove beliefs, habits, attitudes, and emotional hang-ups from our lives and practices. It's like spiritual refinement. God wants to see His own image in our lives and relationships.

It's up to you to realize your value and your position and start walking in it. Your scars no longer own you. See what God sees. It's time for you to look!

Application

1. What spiritual impurities do you need to have removed from your thoughts and actions?
2. How can you see God's refining process not as something to endure but as something that liberates?
3. What beliefs do you hold that may not be based on true knowledge or complete understanding?

Prayer

God, help me to see my challenges as part of Your refining process and help me focus not on the stress of the process but on the joys of the outcome. Amen.

PART 4

THE *GO* OF GIVING UP OUR PURSUITS FOR SOMETHING GREATER

> To Him who is able to do far more abundantly beyond all that we ask or think, according to the power that works with us.
>
> —EPHESIANS 3:20

A little girl was trying to earn money to buy candy. She worked hard doing different chores for her parents. Finally, she earned two dollars. She was ready to head to the candy store with her dad. She knew exactly what she wanted to pick out.

When they arrived, her dad asked her to hold his hand as they walked across the parking lot so she wouldn't accidentally get hurt. But the hand she used to grasp her dad's hand was the same one that held her money. Before she knew it, the wind blew her two dollars out to the road, where cars were driving past.

The little girl instantly tried to let go of her dad's hand to chase her money, but her daddy wouldn't loosen his grip. With no money to buy candy, tears sprang to her eyes. But she soon noticed they kept walking toward the candy store. As they entered, she saw her dad pull a twenty-dollar bill from his pocket. At that moment she realized that being with her father was much more valuable than chasing after what she had worked for and lost.

Many of us have worked hard to achieve our goals. We have pursued our own plans. We've set up our own markers, savings, and hopes. But what God has in His pocket for us is exceedingly and abundantly more than we have ever even dreamed of.

Application

1. When did you pursue something only to discover that God had something even better planned for you? What was it?
2. Do you believe God has plans for you that are "far more abundantly beyond all that [you] ask or think"?
3. How does that knowledge change the way you pursue your goals?

Prayer

Father, thank You that Your goals for me are so much greater than I could ever imagine. Let me pursue what You have planned for me rather than my own goals. Amen.

THE *GO* OF RESPONDING TO GOD'S CALL

> If you belong to Christ, then you are Abraham's descendants, heirs according to promise.
>
> —GALATIANS 3:29

In Genesis 12:1–3, God made a great promise to a man named Abram. This promise gives us insight into how we can get all that God has in store for us as well. It's basically a blueprint.

> The LORD said to Abram, "Go forth from your country, and from your relatives and from your father's house, to the land which I will show you; and I will make you a great nation, and I will bless you, and make your name great; and so you shall be a blessing; and I will bless those who bless you, and the one who curses you I will curse. And in you all the families of the earth will be blessed." (NASB1995)

Go. It's a big word in a small package offering a great promise. That sounds like a bright future with a lasting legacy. As followers of Christ, we are all Abraham's children and heirs to Abraham and his promises. God would not have put us here if He did not have something in store for our lives.

God calls us to go as well. Yet sometimes we remain stuck where we are. That's because while *go* is an easy word to interpret, it's a challenging word to live out.

God has a plan for you based on His kingdom and His agenda. Greatness sits on the precipice of your life, waiting for you to reach out and grab it. Don't forget. You are an heir.

Application

1. Why do you think it is so difficult for some people to go?
2. When have you felt God calling you to go? How did you respond?
3. How might Genesis 12 give you insight into how you can get all that God has in store for you?

Prayer

God, through Christ, I too am a descendant of Abraham and an heir to Your promise. Remind me of that legacy when You call me to go so that I will quickly respond. Amen.

THE *GO* JOURNEY TOWARD GREATNESS

> Let's not become discouraged in doing good, for in
> due time we will reap, if we do not become weary.
>
> —GALATIANS 6:9

It took the woman a week to run a mile without stopping. As the weeks continued, she kept going, running longer and longer. Eventually she ran her first 5K, then a 10K, half marathon, marathon . . . until she had completed a 70.3-mile triathlon. It all started with her first run twelve years before. She kept pushing and didn't stop until she accomplished her goal and experienced victory.

There is always a journey to every victory in life. It isn't just about arriving at the promises. Often, it's the path that shapes, molds, and makes us into the greatness we seek. That runner couldn't show up for a marathon having only run a mile. She had to go on her journey toward greatness.

Greatness is a process. Every victory, success, finish line, concert, or touchdown doesn't happen by luck. Those who pursue the journey appreciate not just a set goal but the work and dedication in accomplishing it.

Many people have not achieved the promises God has for them because they got too caught up chasing their own expectations and failed to focus and follow through on God's journey for them. In Genesis 12, God told Abram to travel from his homeland, his family, and his father's house to the land God would show him before revealing the full extent of His great plan for him. If Abram didn't go, he couldn't achieve greatness. It's that simple.

If you want God's great promises, then it's time to go on that journey toward them.

Application

1. In what areas do you need to strengthen your perseverance and discipline?
2. As you've journeyed toward greatness in God's kingdom, what has been one of the most important lessons you've learned?
3. What steps can you take today to keep going on your journey?

Prayer

Father, forgive me for the times I've grown weary, distracted, and discouraged on my journey. Fill me with perseverance so I can follow wherever You lead. Amen.

THE *GO* OF GETTING UNSETTLED

> Terah took his son Abram, and Lot the son of Haran, his grandson, and his daughter-in-law Sarai, his son Abram's wife, and they departed together from Ur of the Chaldeans to go to the land of Canaan; and they went as far as Haran and settled there.
>
> —GENESIS 11:31

Considering Abram's call from God to go to another land, we often forget that Abram had already settled down. He had a wife and a nice amount of wealth.

Abram's family "went as far as Haran and settled there" (Genesis 11:31). To "go as far as" implies that they still had farther to go. Regardless, they chose to settle. *Settled* is different from *camped*. *Camped* means we're still planning to go somewhere—we're just taking a break. A camp is like a rest station, not a permanent space. But Abram hadn't just camped; Abram had settled. Stopped. Finished. He was good where he was.

But God wasn't. God wasn't good with Abram having gone only "so far" but not all the way into the Promised Land. That's why the word of the Lord came to Abram to unsettle him from the place where he had settled.

God's plan for us and our plans for ourselves are often in two different locations. Just because we are settled and have met our personal goals and reached our life, career, finance, and family expectations doesn't mean that God is okay with it.

When you feel settled, know that God isn't finished with you yet. He has plans for you. So don't get too comfortable—He may unsettle you, and you need to be ready!

Application

1. In what areas do you feel settled and like you have arrived?
2. How do you think you would react if God called you to unsettle in those areas?
3. What steps can you take to prepare yourself for God's unsettling call?

Prayer

God, help me to keep myself prepared for when You call me to unsettle. May I not have a camping mindset but one that is ready to be unsettled for Your purposes. Amen.

THE *GO* OF SEEKING WHAT GOD IS REALLY SAYING TO US

As the heavens are higher than the earth, so are My ways higher than your ways and My thoughts than your thoughts.

—ISAIAH 55:9

Most of us approach God's Word assuming He is telling us what we are already thinking. We want the Bible to rubber-stamp our own thoughts. So we flip through the pages to find the verse that justifies our decisions. But that's not how God works.

Far too often many of us get stuck thinking that when our plans and expectations have been met, God's plans and expectations have been met too. God is not here to reinforce our thoughts or to help us follow our deceitful hearts (Jeremiah 17:9). His thoughts and ways and plans are far beyond ours.

So how do we know when God is really speaking to us through His Word? When God speaks, He is frequently trying to get us to think differently from our normal train of thought. We'll know the direction we're supposed to go is from God when our response is more along the lines of, "Ah, man. C'mon, Jesus, stop!"

What is God saying—more often than not—to us? That He is not finished with us. The game is still going on, and we've got more to do. So when you come upon a passage that causes you to uncomfortably confront something in your life that needs changing, you know He's speaking to you.

Application

1. Have you been guilty of picking and choosing what Scripture passages you want to read to find a "message" that leads you in the direction you want to go?
2. What is the best way to go to the Scriptures?
3. How does understanding that God's thoughts and ways are higher than ours change the way you read Scripture and listen for His voice?

Prayer

God, forgive me for the times I've tried to make You say what I want to hear. Open my ears and my heart to truly hear from You and to obey. Amen.

THE *GO* OF MOVING BEYOND WHERE WE ARE NOW

> [Jesus] said to them, "Follow Me, and I will make you fishers of people."
>
> —MATTHEW 4:19

I had my plan set. I was going to play as a fullback in the NFL for ten years. I'd save all my money. Then I'd get married, have a family, buy a house in a tropical location, and simulcast some teachings with my dad, who is a pastor, while sitting on a beach and experiencing the luxuries of life.

As a Christian, those plans sounded good—I would be able to share Jesus with other people: in my media interviews, on the field, through the simulcasts. But God didn't seem to agree with my plans. I had dreamed up all of this when God grabbed hold of my arm and said, "Stay here with Me. My plan is better than all of that. You just can't see it yet."

In the Bible we see over and over how God gave people a completely different call from what they were expecting. Like Noah building a boat in a world without rain. Or like Ruth becoming a direct ancestor of the Messiah. David wasn't daydreaming of becoming a king as he watched over the sheep. Peter wasn't thinking about becoming an apostle and church leader when he was on his boat fishing. These individuals never considered where God was taking them. This is because God was taking them to a totally different place.

Sometimes God calls us to a completely different path from the one we imagined. But we can trust and follow His leading, for that is where our greatness truly lies.

Application

1. Can you think of someone who has completely switched directions under God's leading? What is their life like now?

2. In what ways has God surprised you by leading you down a path you never expected? What was the outcome?

3. Why is it better to follow God's direction than pursue your own?

Prayer

God, my greatest desire is to trust You more. Wherever You lead, let me be willing to drop everything and follow You. Amen.

THE *GO* OF HOLDING TO THE STANDARD

> Sarai said to Abram, "See now, the Lord has prevented me from bearing children. Please have relations with my slave woman; perhaps I will obtain children through her." And Abram listened to the voice of Sarai.
>
> —GENESIS 16:2

When I played basketball when I was younger, I was focused not just on making points but on dunking the ball. And I was really good—even at five foot three. One day my dad came to the gym and watched me dribble down the court and dunk the ball. I was so proud—until Dad told the athletic director to raise the basket back up to its original position. I'd made him lower it so I could reach my goal easier!

Have you ever wanted something so badly that you lowered the goal to achieve it? You're looking at what you've lost, and you're still trying to come up with ways to go get it. But God won't lower His standard, no matter how much we plead or get frustrated or angry. Because He knows what is best for us and the best way for us to have victory.

Abram was old and still without any children—and God had promised that he would be the father of many nations. How could that be possible if he didn't have a child? So he moved the hoop and tried to "help" God out by having a child through another woman, not his wife. He might have congratulated himself on reaching the goal—just as I did whenever I dunked the ball into the lowered basket—but the reality was that if he wanted true victory, he needed to hold to God's standard.

Application

1. In what areas have you tried to lower the goals?
2. Have you listened to voices other than God's that distract you from His standard?
3. How can you safeguard yourself to maintain God's standard in your life?

Prayer

God, I don't want to move the hoop or lower the goal You have set for my life. I commit to pursuing Your standard. Strengthen my resolve, I pray. Amen.

THE *GO* OF CHANGING YOUR STANCE

Does not wisdom call, and understanding raise her voice? On the top of the heights beside the way, where the paths meet, she takes her stand.

—PROVERBS 8:1-2

When I played in the NFL, our coach was Bill Parcells. One of the first things he did when the players arrived at training camp was to adjust our stance. A stance is the starting position a player takes to get ready for the play to begin, before the ball is snapped. Even though I'd used my stance for more than eight years, Coach wanted to address it. He didn't want us to rely on what had gotten us to that point. Even though our stances may have worked in college and high school, this new level wasn't high school or college. We were playing professional ball. The plays were different. The players were different too. And our stance needed to reflect that.

Some of us need to change our stance in our Christian walk. We need to address how we make our decisions, talk to our spouse or our children, relate to others, serve in the church, or deal with our money. We need to consider how we spend time with God, in His Word, aligning our thoughts under His. We need to change our stance because we're in a whole new league now—it's called the kingdom of God. And it's for serious followers of Jesus.

Ask God how He wants you to change your stance. He wants to make sure you are positioned to retain it and manage it well so you can be ready to give your best in the game.

Application

1. Why do you think God wants us to change our stance when we become Christians?
2. In what areas do you sense God asking you to adjust and change?
3. What are some ways you can follow through on those changes?

Prayer

God, when You ask me to change my stance, help me to be willing and give me the strength I need to change it the way You desire. Amen.

THE *GO* OF LEAVING THINGS BEHIND

> The love of money is a root of all sorts of evil, and some by longing for it have wandered away from the faith and pierced themselves with many griefs.
>
> —1 TIMOTHY 6:10

It's tough to let go of things sometimes, isn't it? Money, possessions, or notoriety can be a strong temptation. Even when God is asking us to let something go, we may cling tightly to it. God is calling us to a higher purpose—a victorious purpose in His kingdom. But to fill that purpose to the fullest, we need to let go and leave some things behind. It may not be money or possessions. We may need to leave our critical thoughts, our will, our history, our hopes, our perspective, our routines, our relationships. If anything we cling to goes against the biblical truth of what God says, we must leave it behind. Drop it. Walk away. That's the only way: give up, *go*, and get what God has given us.

Too many of us want assurance from God that the grass on the other side of the fence is as green—or greener—as where we are standing right now before we go. But the truth is, we must be willing to let go *before* God will show us what He has planned. Yes, it's an uncomfortable feeling. Yes, it's a stretching experience. But isn't that what faith is all about?

Application

1. Have you ever felt God asking you to give something up? How did you respond?

2. What would be the most difficult thing to let go of? How would your feelings about it change if you knew God had something better for you?

3. If you're holding on to something you know goes against God's best for you, what about that thing is difficult to release?

Prayer

God, strengthen me to cling to the things that honor You and let go of the things that dishonor You. Amen.

THE *GO* OF LIVING BY FAITH

> Faith is the certainty of things hoped for, a proof of things not seen. For by it the people of old gained approval.
>
> —HEBREWS 11:1–2

When I was in the twelfth grade, I asked my dad how he overcame so many struggles in his life. He grew up in the rough inner city of Baltimore, raised by a father who was a high school dropout and a mother who for a long time was far from God. How in the world had he become such a great man? I needed to know the secret so I could apply it to my life.

"Go read Hebrews 11 and tell me what you see," he told me.

As I read through that chapter, I noticed a phrase kept popping up over and over. Almost every verse started with "By faith . . ."

I went back to my dad with the answer, but then I asked if having faith meant that I needed to follow my heart.

"Son, I never said that," he replied quickly. "The heart is the most deceitful part of you and is desperately sick. Don't follow your heart. Instead, you live by faith in making your heart follow the truth. Once you learn to do that, you'll be just fine."

Living by faith means making your heart follow God's truth. When your desires, emotions, and responses to what life throws at you pull you one way, make sure you find out what God says about it and follow that. He is waiting for you to *go* by faith. God unleashes greatness on those who live by faith.

Application

1. How would you define faith?
2. In what ways has living by faith given you strength in times of weakness?
3. What are some ways you can build your faith?

Prayer

God, I want a strong and enduring faith that keeps me always in the center of Your approval. Give me that faith that is willing to risk everything for You. Amen.

THE *GO* OF BEING A BLESSING TO OTHERS

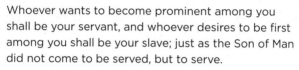

Whoever wants to become prominent among you shall be your servant, and whoever desires to be first among you shall be your slave; just as the Son of Man did not come to be served, but to serve.

—MATTHEW 20:26–28

God told Abraham He would make him a great nation first, then He said He'd make his name great. It wasn't the other way around. It was about the nation. It was about others. Abraham's name would become legendary, yes, but not until God's purpose of using him to bring blessing to others was carried out.

Compare that to the greatness we have in God's kingdom. God is calling each of us to greatness. But His definition of greatness is the exact opposite of the world's definition. It's not all about "me."

Greatness doesn't mean storing up blessings for ourselves. Greatness is all about increasing our influence and strength in such a way that we can become a greater blessing *to others*.

Sure, we are saved for free, but spiritual maturity takes work. Salvation is a gift, but growth is a grind. We have to obey what God tells us to do. His plans for us are bigger than us because they are not just for us.

If we want to be great in God's kingdom, then we must make ourselves less and *go* to serve and help others. We may not see our name in lights because of it—on earth. But in heaven, God sees and will reward with greatness beyond what we could ever imagine.

Application

1. In what ways have you been tempted to put yourself first to gain greatness?
2. As you think about God's definition of greatness, how did Jesus model it best?
3. What specific things can you do to serve others this week?

Prayer

Father, give me Your vision for what greatness really is, and give me opportunities to serve and bless others today. Amen.

THE *GO* OF GIVING YOUR LIFE COMPLETELY TO GOD

Watch yourselves, that you do not lose what we have accomplished, but that you may receive a full reward.

—2 JOHN 1:8

One of my greatest challenges as a chaplain in the Cowboys organization came when one of the players, Jerry Brown, Jr., died in a car accident not long before the team was scheduled to fly to Cincinnati. As I was boarding the plane, Coach Jason Garrett gave me the news. "I need you to do something for the players," he told me.

I prayed with and consoled the guys, and that night for the chapel service, I presented the Gospel to the majority of the team. And, God be praised, a good number of the guys were saved.

Just before the next game, they announced Jerry's death and asked for a moment of silence. As the game started, I turned to the player next to me and asked, "Is this what we're living for? You give years of your best efforts, and all you get in return is a moment. Then the game just continues." The player nodded sadly because he understood.

Hall of Famer or not, the most they're going to give you on this earth is a moment—if you even get that. Why? Because man can't offer anything else. We spend all this time chasing, working, struggling, and striving for worldly greatness, and yet all we get is a moment of silence. That doesn't seem worth it to me. That's why living with an eternal perspective is so important. Because the greatness God has to offer lasts a lot longer than a moment. God gives an eternity of blessing and greatness.

Application

1. Are you living by the world's standards for a moment, or are you living for true greatness?
2. What thing or place or direction is your "go"?
3. If you haven't given God your life and pursuits, what's stopping you?

Prayer

God, I long for more than a moment's praise. I want to be known for being great in serving only You. Amen.

PART 5

DRESS

DRESS TO REFLECT WHO AND WHOSE YOU ARE

As those who have been chosen of God, holy and beloved, put on a heart of compassion, kindness, humility, gentleness, and patience.

—COLOSSIANS 3:12

I remember watching my wife walk down the aisle on our wedding day. She was beautiful, dressed in the perfect wedding gown that she had taken great pains to find for this special day. She understood that what she wore mattered. She would never have considered wearing torn blue jeans, a T-shirt, and flip-flop sandals to this formal and sacred ceremony. And I would never have switched out a tuxedo for something I'd wear to the gym to work out in.

Weddings aren't the only occasions or places where our clothing choices make a difference. We would never think of wearing a wool suit to a beach or a pair of shorts to go ice skating. If graduating or getting an award, we are not going to dress as though we are going to the movies.

A football team's uniform identifies its players. The same is true for hospital staff. Every Tuesday at my church the men wear button-up shirts and a tie. It's the tradition of our "meeting day."

How we dress matters. What we wear reflects where we are headed. It can also reflect who we are. When we give our lives to God, He gives us a new way to dress. But it isn't what we wear on the outside; it's the way we clothe the inside—our hearts. He dresses us with a heart of compassion, kindness, humility, gentleness, and patience.

Ask God to dress you in the attire He has picked for you.

Application

1. Have you ever mis-dressed for an occasion? How did that make you feel?
2. Why is it important for God to give us a new way to dress?
3. In what ways does our heart dressing represent who we are and where we are headed?

Prayer

God, clothe my heart to represent You so that people can see who I represent. Amen.

DRESS FOR WHERE GOD IS LEADING YOU

> The Lord God made garments of skin for Adam and his wife, and clothed them.
>
> —GENESIS 3:21

"Where do you think you're going in that?" Ever heard someone say that? Maybe your parents uttered those words—or a spouse, a friend, a sibling, or even one of your kids. You know exactly what the question really means: *You aren't going anywhere in that. You need to change clothes.*

God said that to Adam and Eve. The couple had sinned and sewn together fig leaves to cover their shame. But when they confessed their sin, God re-dressed them with "garments of skin." What they had sewn together was insufficient in covering their sin. God needed to change their clothes because only He could forgive their sin and cover the shame of their hearts. Their fig leaves were a lame attempt at compensating for the loss of their purity and their place in that paradise garden. He still cared enough about them to make sure their covering would convey His continuing watchfulness and love over their life and future labors.

What does this one short verse have to do with us? He's telling us that *how* we are dressed determines *how far* we go. We too must be dressed with purity. We need to let God cover us with "a garment of skin"—Jesus.

What we wear matters. It means something. It makes a statement. If you want to get what God is giving you, you have to be dressed in connection with how great that purpose, promise, and destiny truly are. Let God clothe you with Jesus.

Application

1. Have you ever had someone comment about what you were wearing? Why did they say about it?
2. Even in the midst of their punishment, God was showing His concern for Adam and Eve. How does this change your perspective of God?
3. What "clothes" are you wearing that may not provide sufficient protection for where God may be leading you?

Prayer

God, where I have sewn fig leaves for myself, re-dress me and cover me with Jesus alone. Amen.

DRESS FOR THE OCCASION

"Friend, how did you get in here without wedding clothes?" And the man was speechless. Then the king said to the servants, "Tie his hands and feet, and throw him into the outer darkness; there will be weeping and gnashing of teeth in that place." For many are called, but few are chosen.

—MATTHEW 22:12–14

Jesus often spoke to His listeners in parables, showing them what the kingdom of heaven was like. In one parable, He alluded to His second coming. The king held a feast to honor his son's marriage. In doing so, the king invited some guests to the reception. But one of the guests showed up in the wrong clothes. The king cornered him and said, "How on earth do you think you're getting in dressed like that?" He turned the man away, sending him to the outer darkness, where there was weeping and gnashing of teeth. Why did he get tossed there? Because the man did not put on the wedding clothes provided for him.

Many people claim to be Christians—they attend church, they do the "right" things and "act" as though they are invited guests, but they aren't dressed properly. They're putting on a good act, but that won't get them into God's kingdom. Jesus ended the parable by announcing that "many are called, but few are chosen." If you want to be chosen, you need to be dressed for the occasion. Wear the clothes of an honored, invited guest, because that is what you are!

Application

1. What does this parable mean to you?
2. Are you dressed properly for the wedding occasion Jesus spoke of? Why or why not?
3. What can help you have the proper attire for Christ's return?

Prayer

God, thank You for clothing me with Christ. May I faithfully wrap myself in His life and love so that I might one day attend the wedding feast of Your Son. Amen.

DRESS TO HONOR WHO YOU'RE WITH

> Do not be conformed to this world, but be transformed by the renewing of your mind, so that you may prove what the will of God is, that which is good and acceptable and perfect.
>
> —ROMANS 12:2

When it comes to dressing, I want to be comfortable. Give me basketball shorts, a T-shirt, a nice pair of Air Jordans, and I'm ready for a date night.

So one evening before our date, my wife, Kanika, turned to me and said, "Time to get dressed."

"Call me when it's about ten minutes till we leave," I told her. I figured that was enough time for me to get ready.

Kanika replied, "We should go ahead and get dressed so we're not late."

After I put on my shorts and shirt, Kanika gave me her look of concern. "Oh, is that what you're wearing?" Then she walked into the closet, picked out a button-up shirt, nice jeans, and dress shoes, then laid them on the bed. "Can you please put this on?"

I soon realized that I needed to dress so that I held her in esteem.

Too many believers dress like heathens. Their outward clothing bears signs and symbols that don't show respect for God. And their inward "clothing" looks more like they're hanging out with the world too much. And God takes one look and says, "You look good to you, and you may look good to other people, but you're not dressed to honor Me." Is what you are wearing honoring the one we're with—Jesus?

Application

1. Have you ever considered that how you dress can send a message of honor to the one you're with?

2. When someone special is with you, do you feel respected to know that they have spent time dressing well to be with you?

3. According to Romans 12:2, how might we dress differently to honor God?

Prayer

God, renew my mind as a beautiful dressing that pleases You. Amen.

DRESS IN AUTHENTICITY

> Our proud confidence is this: the testimony of our
> conscience, that in holiness and godly sincerity, not in
> fleshly wisdom but in the grace of God, we have con-
> ducted ourselves in the world.
>
> —2 CORINTHIANS 1:12

When it comes to being a Christian, we are slowly going down the rabbit hole of finding our value in "looking the part" rather than actually "being the part." We are start-ing to believe, as a culture, that the applause of humanity equals the applause of God. But this is critical to under-stand: The two are not synonymous.

I know men who show up to church dressed to the nines, ready to serve in ministry, who simultaneously do not love their wives. But they'll be at church on time, but-ton up their shirts just right, say their long, super-churchy prayers, join the leadership team, and even become dea-cons. And everyone around them will think they're doing great spiritually. But if we were to sit down and talk with them, as I have, we'd know it's just a cover for their spiri-tual rags. We can't trick God. We've become professionals at wearing costumes and facades that impress the world, all the while ignoring the fact that God is not fooled or impressed.

If we want to please God and have victory in our lives, then it's time for us to get rid of the costumes and facades and dress our lives and attitudes with authenticity.

Application

1. As you look at the closet of your heart, are you dressing so the world will be pleased or are you dressing to be authentic with God and with others?
2. Do you work to get people to follow you more than you get them to follow Christ?
3. In what ways can you dress to be more authentic this week?

Prayer

Father, forgive me for the ways I try to hide who I really am when You're calling me to live a life of authenticity. Fill me with Your strength so I can please You. Amen.

DRESS FOR SIMPLICITY

> I am afraid that, as the serpent deceived Eve by his craftiness, your minds will be led astray from the simplicity and purity of devotion to Christ.
>
> —2 CORINTHIANS 11:3 NASB1995

Fig leaves are large, strong leaves. They aren't easily torn, and they look good. These were the leaves Adam and Eve chose for their clothes.

A lot of times we choose big things—our own fig leaves—to cover our insecurities. We show everyone our house, if it's large. We show everyone our car, if it's valuable. We show everyone pictures of us working out, if we're strong. We give impressions of what we know (or think) will impress. Why? Because it makes us feel better about ourselves, just as Adam and Eve tried to feel better about themselves all dressed up in their fig leaves. They were covered, but deep down they still felt shame. They were dressed, but they still felt discouraged, depressed, and on their own.

Bigger isn't better; bigger won't cover our insecurity and shame and won't protect our minds from the evil one. What we need to pursue instead is simplicity and a clear focus on Jesus. When we feel insecure and become tempted to dress big, instead let us go to the God who knows how to cover us with pure devotion and simplicity in Jesus.

Application

1. How often have you felt the need to go bigger with something in your life? What do you think is really at the root of that desire?
2. What might God be leading you to give up in order to more fully pursue Him?
3. In what ways could dressing for simplicity require courage? Why?

Prayer

Father, help me to pursue You above all so I can find the peace and contentment I long for. Amen.

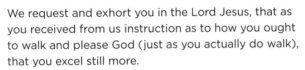

DRESS IN THE COVERING OF OBEDIENCE

> We request and exhort you in the Lord Jesus, that as you received from us instruction as to how you ought to walk and please God (just as you actually do walk), that you excel still more.
>
> —1 THESSALONIANS 4:1 NASB1995

When Adam and Eve were obedient, they were naked but unashamed. They felt the covering of obedience. When they were disobedient, they were clothed but ashamed. They recognized just how naked they really were.

There is a covering of protection that is simply tied to faith in Christ and allegiance to His overarching rule in our lives. It's embedded in obedience. Faith in Christ saves us, but once we add disobedience to the equation of our relationship with God, we get that naked feeling again. Once we see our wrongful actions boomerang right back to slap us in the face, we feel naked and vulnerable. We may temporarily enjoy what the world has to offer, but we're simultaneously running from what God wants to give.

Obedience covers us and keeps us safe. Knowing that, we shouldn't just obey, but as Paul exhorts us, we should "excel still more" in our pursuit to obey. If we want to experience greatness and the full benefits of our faith, then we must respond to God's call on our lives with obedience. What a great and wonderful protective covering that will provide us!

Application

1. Are you in a situation where you know God is asking for obedience from you, and yet you are struggling with it?
2. Has there been a time when you humbly obeyed God even when you didn't want to?
3. When you obeyed God despite your initial resistance, what happened that brought fruit out of it?

Prayer

God, help me to live a life of purity and wholeness that will create a greatness within me. Soften my heart and mind to excel even more in following Your desires for me. Amen.

DRESS WITH YOUR HAND IN HIS

> When he falls, he will not be hurled down, because the LORD is the One who holds his hand.
>
> —PSALM 37:24

Our son Kamden has always had a strong will and abundant energy—he was walking before he was eight months old. When he was a toddler, I taught him to walk down the stairs. I grabbed hold of his hand so he couldn't get down on his own. But as we descended together one step at a time, he continuously attempted to yank his hand free of my grip.

I wanted to teach Kamden a lesson that would help him in the long run. With one step left, I released him. Kamden tumbled down that one final stair. He landed right on his bottom, all because he insisted on going it alone, going his own way.

Sometimes we want to go our own way. So God lets go of our hand, and we fall flat on our bottoms too. Thus we learn not to yank away from Him and His will.

Every time after that, Kamden reached out his hand to grab mine before going down the stairs. And it's the same way with us. We find ourselves vulnerable because we've yanked ourselves away from God's hand. But if we'll just turn around, we'll see His hand still there, ready to cover us with His hand of dressing, the same hand that created us from dust, clothed us in Christ, and wants to clothe us in greatness. Hold His hand, and be clothed in what He knows to be best.

Application

1. When have you pulled away from God to do things your own way? What happened?
2. What might holding on to God's hand look like in your everyday routines?
3. How do you know when You've pulled away from God's hand?

Prayer

Father, when I am tempted to go my own way, open my eyes to see Your loving, strong, protective hand held out to me. Amen.

DRESS IN THE GARMENTS OF SALVATION

> I will rejoice greatly in the Lord, my soul will be joyful in my God; for He has clothed me with garments of salvation, He has wrapped me with a robe of righteousness, as a groom puts on a turban, and as a bride adorns herself with her jewels.
>
> —ISAIAH 61:10

Adam and Eve recognized they had been created for righteousness precisely because of their sin. They realized their shame because of the shamelessness they had once known. They knew they had to be covered in order to feel secure and protected, because they had felt secure and protected by God himself.

When we see spiritual darkness and sin all around us, we know that we've been created for righteousness. We've been created to make a difference for good in this land— and that good comes only through Christ. We must clothe ourselves in His righteousness.

The first sacrifice was in the garden. God sacrificed an innocent animal and took its skin to clothe Adam and Eve—a constant reminder that an innocent animal died in their place.

Likewise, we are covered with the shed blood of Jesus Christ. Our lifestyle should reflect His sacrifice made on our behalf. The only reason you and I are here today is because we are a living testimony of the innocent Lamb who was slain.

As I consider the truth of how Christ's sacrifice covers me, I know that the only way I can move forward and go to the place where God is calling me is to wear the "garments of salvation" and the "robe of righteousness."

Application

1. In your life, what does wearing the robe of righteousness look like?
2. In what ways can you attract others to Christ by the garments of salvation that you wear?
3. How can you better dress yourself under God's covering?

Prayer

God, give me a heart that longs to please only You and teach me to practice righteousness. Amen.

DRESS IN THE FULL ARMOR OF GOD

> Put on the full armor of God, so that you will be able to stand firm against the schemes of the devil.
>
> —EPHESIANS 6:11

Once we claim Christ as our Lord and Savior, Satan puts a target out on our lives. It's all-out war, and we are in a spiritual battle. There's nothing he hates more than Christians who live out their purpose and seize their victory and the promises of God.

We wear the garment of salvation and the robe of righteousness, which identify us as belonging to God as His faithful followers. But we have another important outfit we need so we can "stand firm against the schemes of the devil." This uniform consists of the full armor of God. This whole-body armor identifies us as servants on mission for Christ. As such we are trying to rescue those in bondage to sin by fighting those spiritual forces that are holding them captive.

Let's look at what that includes: the belt of truth, the breastplate of righteousness, shoes of peace, the shield of faith, the helmet of salvation, and the sword of the Spirit, which is the Word of God. Five of the items are strictly protective. But with the sword, we can counter the lies of the enemy and take the offense to defeat them and release the captives we are trying to help.

These are all practical ways we can dress for spiritual warfare. Because when God calls us, He wants us to be ready to do battle—and win.

Application

1. What steps can you take today to persevere in the battle?
2. In what ways will you align your heart with God's Word today?
3. What might each piece of armor look like in your interactions this week?

Prayer

God, You have given me the exact clothes I need to dress for victory and to live out my purpose. Let me never grow weary of wearing the armor that will always save my life from the fiery arrows of the enemy. Amen.

PART 6

CONFIDENCE

THE *THEREFORE* THAT PROVIDES CONFIDENCE

> Therefore let's approach the throne of grace with confidence, so that we may receive mercy and find grace for help at the time of our need.
>
> —HEBREWS 4:16

What do you think of when you hear the word *confidence*? Do you think of someone who has it all together? Do you think of Tom Brady with two minutes left, down by a few points, at the Super Bowl? Do you think of the images of perfect-looking people you scroll past on social media? Confidence means a lot of different things to different people. But if you were to peel back the veneer of what our world defines as *confidence*, you'd find it's often just a mask. It's just an image to hide an insecurity. Or it's just a motivation to avoid failure. Having known celebrities and elite athletes personally, I can tell you this truth firsthand.

Confidence often camouflages uncertainty.

But not for those who follow Jesus. Because we know the end of the story, we know what comes after the heartache and disappointments of this life. The biblical writers often expressed that confidence this way: by using the word *for*.

It's another way of saying *because*. Or a word often used to prove a point such as *thus* or *hence*. Sometimes they would lengthen it to *therefore*. However we want to say it, it means the same thing: that we are confident of what comes after it—that we can approach God, knowing that He will compassionately offer us help when we need it.

Application

1. Have you ever thought about the word *for* indicating that you can be confident of what comes after?
2. What does having that kind of confidence mean for you?
3. How might you live differently today with that understanding?

Prayer

Lord, thank You that I can boldly approach You, knowing without a shadow of a doubt that You will bless me with Your mercy and will provide help—always and whenever I need it. That gives me confidence as I live each day. Amen.

THE *THEREFORE* THAT KNOWS WHO TO PUT YOUR CONFIDENCE IN

For the Lord will be your confidence, and will keep your foot from being caught.

—PROVERBS 3:26

Have you ever put your confidence in someone only to have them disappoint you? Perhaps it was a parent, an athlete, or your favorite teacher. You put confidence in that person and placed them on a pedestal, and then the pedestal crumbled and crashed. It's especially painful when you put your confidence in a pastor or renowned spiritual leader only to discover that the person failed in some way. They didn't have it all together like you thought. The truth is that people are always going to let us down, because they're human.

Or maybe you put your confidence in yourself only to discover that you weren't all you thought you were. It's a tough letdown, isn't it?

There's One who will never let us down, however. Only when we put our confidence in God will we never be disappointed. The Bible reminds us of this repeatedly:

- Therefore let's approach the throne of grace with confidence, so that we may receive mercy and find grace for help at the time of our need. (Hebrews 4:16)
- We confidently say, "The Lord is my helper, I will not be afraid. What will man do to me?" (Hebrews 13:6)
- This is the confidence which we have before Him, that, if we ask anything according to His will, He hears us. (1 John 5:14)

Those are some pretty big claims. But we serve a really big God—who can back all of them up. And that's definitely Someone we can always be confident in.

Application

1. Why do you think it's so disappointing when people fail to live up to the confidence we put in them?
2. Who in your life did you place confidence in and then they let you down?
3. How did you feel when that person fell off your pedestal?

Prayer

Father, You are steadfast and true, always keeping Your word, always watching out for me. Thank You that I can trust You fully and completely. Amen.

THE *THEREFORE* THAT OFFERS ASSURANCE

> Being fully assured that what God had promised, He was able also to perform.
>
> —ROMANS 4:21

Going into the 1972 Munich Olympics, Great Britain's distance runner David Bedford, ranked number one in the world, was expected to take home the gold medal. But finishing in sixth place in the 10,000-meter run, he set his eyes on the 5,000-meter. After four laps, apparently weighed down by expectation, Bedford choked, lost heart, and finished in twelfth place.

People say that an athlete or a team who seems to lack confidence "chokes" at the end of a game or race. Lack of confidence in themselves and in each other shows up in what they do and how they play. They may stand and even look like they are confident. But they know it's an empty effort.

True confidence doesn't need to be displayed. It requires no bravado. It just shows up in the consistency of the one who has it in order to do the right thing, make the play, secure the deal, ride out the storm, or maneuver through life's difficulties and challenges. This kind of confidence can also be biblically defined as *assurance*. Hebrews 11:1

puts it like this: "Now faith is the assurance of things hoped for, the conviction of things not seen" (NASB1995). In other words, it is a conviction that what we believe to be true *is* true. That level of assurance always affects our actions, so we never have to choke.

Application

1. Have you ever choked when facing something important? What happened? Why did you choke?
2. What do you think when you see other people choke?
3. How does having assurance in your faith affect your actions every day?

Prayer

Lord, thank You that I never have to worry about not being able to handle what You've set before me, for I know that You will give me the strength to carry out Your will. Amen.

THE *THEREFORE* THAT LEADS TO TRUSTING GOD WILL CHANGE YOU

> For I am confident of this very thing, that He who began a good work among you will complete it by the day of Christ Jesus.
>
> —PHILIPPIANS 1:6

Did you know that art historians lovingly refer to the famous artist Leonardo da Vinci as a "brilliant slacker"? He was notorious for abandoning projects when he became disenchanted. In 1481, some Augustinian monks commissioned him to paint *The Adoration of the Magi*, which depicted the wise men surrounding the baby Jesus. He never completed it, instead turning his attention halfway through to paint *The Last Supper*. Have you ever known someone to give up halfway through their work? They become disenchanted or distracted or bored. Or perhaps you've given up on a project, and there it sits in a corner week after week.

But God isn't like that. He completes what He starts. He created us as His masterpieces (see Ephesians 2:10) and has every intention of completing what He has begun in us.

The apostle Paul is so certain of this truth that he starts his sentence with that confident word *for*: "*For* I am confident of this very thing . . ."

He wants us to sit in the power of this principle. He is encouraging us to take a deep breath because of this reality. He wants us to know that God *will* perfect what He started in everyone who trusts Him. Don't despair when you struggle and feel as though you're never going to be the great person you were meant to be. Be assured, God isn't finished with you yet. He doesn't do things halfway.

Application

1. Have you ever given up on a project halfway? Why?
2. What do you think when you see others abandon projects?
3. How does it make you feel to know that God will never abandon His work on you—no matter what?

Prayer

Lord, thank You for creating me with a purpose and helping me fulfill that. I praise You for giving me that confidence! Amen.

THE *THEREFORE* OF MISPLACED CONFIDENCE

Instruct those who are rich in this present world not to be conceited or to set their hope on the uncertainty of riches, but on God, who richly supplies us with all things to enjoy.

—1 TIMOTHY 6:17

In the 2008 recession, many people lost their savings and stock portfolios. People who had confidently planned for retirement now found themselves facing foreclosures and repossessions and having to start again from scratch. Some experienced such anxiety and depression over their losses that they took their own lives. They had misplaced their confidence—placing their hope and trust in the things of this world rather than the Creator of this world.

These misplaced assurances are nothing new. Even the apostle Paul warned a young Timothy to help believers make sure they placed their expectations and confidence in the right things.

A lot of times we experience unmet expectations or get thrown off track in life, not because God is misplaced but because our confidence is misplaced. Sometimes our confidence is in things that cannot be held responsible for the valuable beliefs we're giving to the object of our confidence. When we place our confidence in anything other than God, we are giving that thing the status of a god.

Putting all of our eggs in any basket other than in God himself will do only one thing for us: teach us not to do that again. Because when it fails, we'll realize that in the spiritual life, it is only God who deserves and has earned our confidence.

Application

1. When have you placed your confidence in something other than God for your security or future? Why?
2. Why is it wrong to place trust in earthly riches rather than in God's riches?
3. According to 1 Timothy 6:17, what does God do for those who place their confidence in Him?

Prayer

God, help me to prioritize my confidence in You so that I don't make earthly riches or pursuits my god. You alone deserve that place. Amen.

THE *THEREFORE* OF MISPLACED RESPONSIBILITY

For to this end I also wrote, so that I might put you to the test, whether you are obedient in all things.

—2 CORINTHIANS 2:9

One day, after plopping down on my comfy couch to watch college football, I decided to give my five-year-old son Kamden my phone to plug in, since my battery was almost out and I was feeling too lazy to do it myself. He focused intently on me and nodded while I explained my instructions. So I confidently handed him my phone.

When I later went to retrieve my phone, it wasn't where it was supposed to be. I found Kamden playing and asked where my phone was. He didn't know because he had gotten distracted and forgot.

Then my wife, Kanika, stepped in. "You gave something valuable to someone who is irresponsible, and now you're mad at him when you never should have given it to him to begin with. He's five years old. He's not the problem." And she was right.

A lot of times that's just what we do. God asks us to do something. Then we resist and give it to somebody else to take care of, feeling confident that they'll handle it—when it wasn't their responsibility in the first place. Then we get mad when things don't work out, or when people aren't doing what we wanted them to. But we're mad for all the wrong reasons. They aren't the problem, we are. We asked them to do or be something that wasn't their responsibility. God gave that responsibility to us. He wants us to be obedient in all things—that includes doing the things He's asked us to do.

Application

1. When have you given something valuable to someone who disappointed you?
2. How can misplaced responsibility come back on you?
3. Have you given something to somebody that God asked you to do? Why?

Prayer

Father, give me Your strength to step into my responsibility and follow You, for Your name's sake. Amen.

THE *THEREFORE* THAT ALL THINGS WILL WORK TO THE GOOD

We know that God causes all things to work together for good to those who love God, to those who are called according to His purpose. For those whom He foreknew, He also predestined to become conformed to the image of His Son, so that He would be the first-born among many brothers and sisters.

—ROMANS 8:28–29

You probably have verse 28 memorized. It's a great and comforting verse. But few ever quote verse 29. It's a *for* verse. These two verses together provide a bigger, more confident picture of God working all things for good. We can be confident *because* He foreknew us, He predestined us—so He already knows it's all going to work out!

Those He predestined, He already called. Those He called, He already justified. Those He justified, He glorified. That's why we can say that when God is for us, who in the world can be against us?

If God is for you, who can be against you? Now, some may rise up to appear as though they are against you. If God is for you, you don't need to be tripping over the situation you are going through. You can be confident that

God will work it out. If God is for you, you don't need to be anxious about the challenge you are facing. If God is for you, you don't need to worry about the circumstances and trials that test you. Because if you have faith in Jesus, you can let go of any fears for your future.

Application

1. Why is it important not to worry about troubles and trials?
2. When have you seen God cause all things to work for good in a situation you faced?
3. How can you think differently about your trials in light of Romans 8:28–29?

Prayer

God, make me ever mindful of my purpose so that I can confidently cling to the promise that You are always working good out of my troubles. Amen.

THE *THEREFORE* OF KNOWING THE OUTCOME

[Jesus said,] "These things I have spoken to you so that in Me you may have peace. In the world you have tribulation, but take courage; I have overcome the world."

—JOHN 16:33

When watching football during the off season, I turn to *NFL Replay*. The difference with viewing these games is that I already know the outcomes. Therefore, I'm able to view the games with a whole different level of confidence.

That's why if a team gets an interception, I don't fuss. If a player fumbles, I don't get worried. If someone on the team I'm cheering for misses a tackle, I don't sulk. If I already know the score and I already know my team won, then why would I get caught up in the problems along the way? I can watch the game with confidence because I already know how it finishes.

This is the kind of confidence we have when we get saved and follow Jesus. We know we ultimately win. So Jesus tells us not to worry. "Chill," He says. "Settle down. I got this."

No matter how bad the news, or what's going down in the culture, you don't have to wring your hands and fret.

Even when the fumbles, interceptions, or missed tackles in the game of your life show up, you can relax because you already know who the Overcomer truly is. So take courage; be confident. He who is *in you* (Colossians 1:27) is greater and has overcome the world.

Application

1. How is watching a game and knowing the outcome different from watching it in real time?
2. In what ways do you look at and respond to life differently knowing the outcome of the world—that we win?
3. What obstacle in your life is God inviting you to look at from the perspective of being an overcomer?

Prayer

God, when I begin to forget life's outcome, remind my heart and mind that You are in control and that You've got this. Amen.

THE *THEREFORE* OF PURSUING GREATNESS

> Every place on which the sole of your foot steps, I have given it to you.
>
> —JOSHUA 1:3

After Moses died, the people needed a new leader—and God already had him picked out: Joshua. God entrusted His people to Joshua to get them safely into the Promised Land. I love this story. One part of Joshua's life that stands out to me most is when God told him that every place he stepped, God was giving that spot to him. Everywhere Joshua went, he was already assured of the victory. Everywhere Joshua walked, it was his to have. He had already been blessed. He had already gotten the victory. He had already been told how his game would wind up. Why wouldn't he walk with confidence? Why wouldn't he be willing to go with whatever route God called him to, no matter how weird it might have sounded? Joshua knew the outcome, so he went out and got all that God had planned for him.

God has called you too. If you find yourself insecure in God's purpose for you and feel tempted to shrink away from His call on your life, know that He will give you the strength to rise to the occasion. You were made for greatness. Now go out and walk those steps confidently, for the God who sustained Joshua and so many others through the Bible and history will sustain you too.

Application

1. What keeps you from believing you can step into the greatness God has called you to?
2. What does the Bible say about who you are in Jesus?
3. How does knowing that God has already given you the victory build confidence in your steps?

Prayer

God, with each step I take, remind me that You have gone before me and have already given me the victory. So fill me with Your confidence as I walk forward. Amen.

THE *THEREFORE* OF REMEMBERING GOD'S SOVEREIGNTY

Remember the former things long past, for I am God, and there is no other; I am God, and there is no one like Me, declaring the end from the beginning, and from ancient times things which have not been done, saying, "My plan will be established, and I will accomplish all My good pleasure."

—ISAIAH 46:9-10

As we walk into our purpose and God's plans for our victory, freedom, and greatness, we must never overlook or forget His sovereignty. God *will* accomplish all of His purposes. Our future is in His sovereign hands. And His plans, His accomplishments through us, are for His good pleasure—which will fill us with blessings.

God is not a mean taskmaster. He does not force His way on us. He doesn't curse us. He is filled with love for us and blesses us—that is His sovereign desire and choice.

As pastor and classic theological author A. W. Pink once wrote, "To the one who delights in the sovereignty of God the clouds not only have a 'silver lining' but they are silvern all through, the darkness only serving to offset the light."* Don't neglect His sovereignty in your life. Rely on it. God hears and acts on your behalf. Remember how He has heard and acted on behalf of His people throughout history. He is the same yesterday, today, and forever.

Application

1. What does delighting in the sovereignty of God mean to you?
2. In what ways does your confidence build with the knowledge that God is sovereign and is watching out for you?
3. What Bible stories can you use to remind you of God's sovereignty and His delight in you?

Prayer

God, You are sovereign over all things, including me. I pray that Your plans for me will be accomplished in my life. Help me to accept your will and confidently move forward in it. Amen.

*Arthur W. Pink, *The Sovereignty of God* (Blacksburg, VA: Wilder Publications, 2008), 179.

THE *THEREFORE* OF CHRIST'S GOOD WORK

> He made Him who knew no sin to be sin on our behalf, so that we might become the righteousness of God in Him.
>
> —2 CORINTHIANS 5:21 NASB1995

What is it that God wants to bring about in us? It's the good news—the Gospel of Jesus Christ. God sent His own Son to live a perfect life, then die on the cross and resurrect three days later. He did this for me and you so that we would become righteous. Now, if we're saved, we might be scratching our heads and wondering what this means. It means the good works we will do are not reliant on us. Jesus will bring them about when we have placed our hopes and our faith in Him. It takes the pressure off of us.

In Exodus 20, God gave the Israelites the Ten Commandments. These commandments outlined what every sinner needed to do in order to be in a right relationship with God. But as you and I know, no one can obey those laws perfectly. So He sent His Son, Jesus Christ, to live out the perfect standard of God's law.

You'll find as you read the Gospels that Jesus came to fulfill the law so that God's standard could be satisfied and that we could become righteous. The sacrificial death and miraculous resurrection of Jesus let us know that the price has been paid in full. As a result, we get to experience His perfection in this life. We don't get the death that we deserve because He died in our place. His good work sets the marker for all of our good works to come.

Application

1. In what way did Jesus fulfill the Law and the Prophets?
2. According to 2 Corinthians 5:21, what are we in Christ?
3. When the enemy tempts you to believe that you are not good enough, what confidence do you have to help you respond?

Prayer

Father, it amazes me that Christ died so that in Him we can be righteous. You have truly given me good news. Amen.

THE *THEREFORE* OF BEING SANCTIFIED

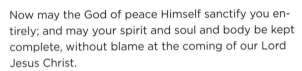

> Now may the God of peace Himself sanctify you entirely; and may your spirit and soul and body be kept complete, without blame at the coming of our Lord Jesus Christ.
>
> —1 THESSALONIANS 5:23

Jesus has freely given us salvation, just for believing. He has justified us. *Justification* means the verdict has been rendered on our behalf. It refers to the judge looking at us and declaring that we are justified, not guilty, free to go.

God wants us to be saved, but He also wants us to be sanctified. *Sanctification* is just a seminary-style word that means "spiritual growth." God has paid the price for our sins through the blood of Jesus Christ, and now He turns His attention to making us into the likeness of Christ.

While we do nothing but accept God's gift of justification, the process of being sanctified requires our cooperation and participation. And while it requires us to act, God assures us He will see us through. So we must focus on matching up our salvation to our lifestyle. We do this by aligning our thoughts, decisions, words, desires, and ambitions with Christ's.

You might be thinking, *How long is this gonna take?*

My answer is the same as Paul's in Philippians 1:6: It's going to take as long as until "the day of Christ Jesus." That's why we should never quit. Because God will continue His work in us until the moment we take our last breath. One victory isn't enough. One great play isn't enough. It's our role now to work out what God has already worked in.

If God has already done so much by saving you, there are no limits to what God wants to do both in and through you for His kingdom and His glory.

Application

1. What's the difference between justification and sanctification?
2. Why do you need both?
3. What is your role in being sanctified?

Prayer

Father, thank You that You continue to shape me to look, act, and be more like Christ. Let me always be a willing participant. Amen.

THE *THEREFORE* OF WORKING OUT YOUR SALVATION

Just as you have always obeyed, not as in my presence only, but now much more in my absence, work out your own salvation with fear and trembling.

—PHILIPPIANS 2:12

One of the most important determining factors in a patient's recovery during physical therapy is their willingness to participate in the process. It requires the patient, even if in pain, to push through and cooperate with the therapist to make any kind of progress. Recovery comes through connection with the one trained to help us recover.

Similarly, you and I can't just sit back and assume Jesus is going to do all the work for us in our spiritual lives. In order to get what God has for us and seize our time right now, we have to put in the work.

Far too many people don't want to put in the work to make a house into a home. Far too many people want a wedding and don't want to do what is necessary to make a marriage. Far too many people want a career and don't want to give the effort to make it a calling. But God is saying, *If you want what I have given to you, you've got to cooperate with Me to perfect My work in you. Stop trying to perfect it on your own. Stop trying to manipulate it into your version of Christian success. Stop pursuing the world's way to gain what I am giving you.*

God will perfect His work in you, but He'll only do it if you partner with Him.

Application

1. In what ways have you tried to "work out your own salvation" on your own?
2. Why do we need God's help in the work?
3. In what specific areas are you struggling in being sanctified?

Prayer

God, I desperately need Your guidance, strength, and wisdom as I strive with my new heart to fulfill my greatest desire to become the image of Jesus. Fill me with a desire to do my part. Amen.

THE *THEREFORE* OF REMAINING CONNECTED

> I am the vine, you are the branches; the one who re-mains in Me, and I in him bears much fruit, for apart from Me you can do nothing.
>
> —JOHN 15:5

If you were playing basketball with the 1990s' Chicago Bulls team and you found yourself down with time for only one more shot in the game, what would you do? Wouldn't you look to pass the ball to Michael Jordan, who could take the shot and win? Of course you would! You know that he would make the shot!

Now, if you are facing detours or dead ends over and over on your spiritual path, are you holding on to the ball too long? Do you need to pass it to Jesus? Paul declared that Jesus will make the shot every time. You just need to give Him the ball and cooperate as He guides your purpose this side of heaven.

Jesus explains it with a vineyard analogy: He is the vine and we are the branches. Vines supply all the nutrition to the branches. That's how they bear fruit. We will bear fruit and shine in life if we learn this art of connecting. Passing the ball. Abiding. Cooperating. Focusing. Trusting. Obeying.

Connect to Him. Trust the power He provides. He's got you. Follow His lead. He knows what He's doing, and He knows what He's asking you to do. Be confident that you will finish; you will win. Because this is what you are saved *for*.

Application

1. Have you ever considered that you have not only been saved *from* but saved *for*? How does that affect your daily life?
2. What might still be holding you back from living confidently in the life God has called you to?
3. What steps can you take to become more confident and remain connected to Christ, the Vine?

Prayer

Father, I have given You my life completely, and I ask You to do with it as You please. Keep me connected to You and confident in my living. Amen.

PART 7

THE *WAIT* OF A COCOON SEASON

> What is my strength, that I should wait? And what is
> my end, that I should endure?
>
> —JOB 6:11

There are times for an athlete when things shut down around them. It's usually when they get an injury and have to go into rehab. My friend Dak Prescott, quarterback for the Dallas Cowboys, knows this all too well. During one game he suffered an excruciating ankle injury. In one moment, everything changed for him. He was going to have to stop playing for a while. And a new focus began: healing and growth.

Players often call this a cocoon season. It's a time to regroup and reset. A caterpillar goes into a cocoon because a transformation needs to take place. That caterpillar may experience isolation and pain, but the opportunity for greater growth can come out of it.

At times we too must go into a cocoon season. Perhaps we've been injured in some way and we need to spend time in healing and growth. As a player in a cocoon season, we get more time to study the playbook. We are able to watch more game film so we can figure out what our opponent is really up to. A cocoon season can give a greater currency than playing at times, and that currency is *time*. In the cocoon, you have time you didn't have when you were on the field or in the grind. You now have reallocated time to assess things about yourself and the players around you. Being in the cocoon may be frustrating and painful, but it also grants you the time to level up. It's not the time to sit, sulk, and sour. It's time to prepare yourself for your breakout moment.

Application

1. Have you experienced a cocoon season you didn't want to be in?
2. What is the benefit to being in a cocoon season?
3. What can you learn about transformation from being in a cocoon season?

Prayer

Lord, give me the eyes to see the importance of a cocoon season so I can use that time wisely. Amen.

THE *WAIT* THAT PROGRESSES THE GOSPEL

I want you to know, brothers and sisters, that my circumstances have turned out for the greater progress of the gospel.

—PHILIPPIANS 1:12

Wait. Pause. Stop. Hold on. *Stuck. Check yourself. Chill.* We know these words well—especially after living through the COVID-19 pandemic of 2020. At first, the lockdown had me feeling down. I wanted and needed to do things and go places, but I couldn't, because everything came to a screeching halt. Thoughts ran through my mind of the various things I was losing or missing out on because everything had shut down.

And yet, as the lockdown continued, I began to see good accomplished. Many of us, including me, refocused our energies and purpose on the most important things in life. Paul learned this same truth, except in a different situation: His life was on pause because he was in prison. And that lockdown also brought about a greater good:

. . . The greater progress of the gospel, so that my imprisonment in the cause of Christ has become well known throughout the praetorian guard and to everyone else, and that most of the brothers and sisters, trusting in the Lord because of my imprisonment, have far more courage to speak the word of God without fear. (Philippians 1:12–14)

He's letting us know that his circumstances were not for nothing. He is comforting us with his own comfort in saying that what he has gone through was not just random or by chance. No, his misery was meaningful and his circumstances were consequential because they turned out for the greater progress of the Gospel of Jesus Christ. May we be able to say the same of our own lockdown experiences when we're forced to wait.

Application

1. Do you wait well?
2. What was the outcome of Paul's wait?
3. What steps can you take during a wait to make progress for the Gospel?

Prayer

God, expand my vision so I can see beyond what I can't do to look for ways to make progress for the Gospel. Amen.

THE *WAIT* THAT BRINGS SOMETHING GREATER

We also celebrate in our tribulations, knowing that tribulation brings about perseverance; and perseverance, proven character; and proven character, hope; and hope does not disappoint.

—ROMANS 5:3-5

You know what it's like to be in a situation you can't alter. Your hands are tied. You are stuck. You want to manipulate the situation with your own hands, but you can't. Your money, friends, family, clout, or charm can't fix it. Not this one. Not this time. It's an emotional, spiritual, or circumstantial lockdown of sorts that no one can do anything about.

In situations like this, Paul has wise insight for us. He wants us to know that the circumstances and troubles we are experiencing, as dark as they may seem, will produce light.

We learn from Paul that if we don't understand and cooperate with the program at hand, our pain will become a bit more painful. Why? Because we'll think that what we are struggling with is only about running us into the ground. We won't realize it's about creating something in ourselves and in others. If we continue thinking our circumstances are for nothing, then our situation will have to continue until it accomplishes what it was put there to produce, and it will take longer to do so. That means a longer *wait*.

No matter how difficult your challenges may seem, they will never be more than what God wants to produce from them. No matter how long you feel you are waiting, God has a goal in mind. God's goal in your purpose will be greater than anything you experienced in your pain. Stay focused on the purpose, rather than the wait.

Application

1. When have you experienced a wait that lasted longer than you expected?
2. In what ways does God use our wait to grow us?
3. How can you specifically stay focused on the purpose rather than the wait today?

Prayer

Lord, give me the vision to see clearly to stay focused on the purpose in the wait instead of the wait itself. Amen.

THE *WAIT* THAT CALLS FOR ENDURANCE

> You have need of endurance, so that when you have done the will of God, you may receive what was promised.
>
> —HEBREWS 10:36

"When is this wait going to be *over already*?"

It's brutal to wait, isn't it? Especially when the wait seems to go on and on. But that just means we have to keep holding on, staying steadfast, and enduring, because one thing's for sure: If it's not good yet, God is not done yet.

If you don't see the good God is producing yet, buckle up, because it isn't over. If you hang in there and trust what He needs to do in your life, you will see the good changes. But if you bail, you'll get both the pain and the purposelessness that come from living outside of God's will. You may not get to choose getting out of the wait, but you *do get* to choose how you will reside in it. Will you have a good attitude? Will you focus on the good God is working in you?

Too many people fail to seize their time in the wait because they fail to grasp the truth of what God is doing. As a result, they throw in the towel before they ever get to have what God intended for them. God doesn't want you to give up. You may find yourself with bumps and bruises during the waiting period. But if you choose to stick with it and finish the course, you'll see what ultimate good God can produce from it.

Application

1. When have you been tempted to quit rather than wait something out?
2. How can keeping a good attitude change an outcome?
3. What one thing can you do today to help you through a time of waiting—or prepare you for when one comes?

Prayer

God, whenever I experience a long period of waiting, let me embrace it instead of fighting against it so that I can see it for what it really is—something to produce good in me. Amen.

THE *WAIT* OF BUILDING A DEEP FOUNDATION

Unless the Lord builds a house, they who build it labor in vain.

—PSALM 127:1

My dad used to take me to downtown Dallas when I was a kid, and we would walk the streets. Anytime we passed a construction site that had been taped off due to a building project, he would walk with me over to the tape and ask me to look down at what they were digging. "How deep is that, Son?" he'd ask. Then he would remind me that a tall building needed a deep and strong foundation.

A lot of people want a skyscraper kind of life but on a chicken-coop foundation. They don't want to do the work of digging deep spiritually, emotionally, and circumstantially. They just want to lay down a few boards or pour one bag of concrete and call it a day. But skyscrapers don't work that way. And neither does God.

God allows the situations in your life to be deep so that He can take you high. When He wants to do a great work in someone, and that someone happens to be you, you better hang on for the ride, because if a skyscraper is going to be eighty stories high, it'll need a foundation that can support it. And building that kind of foundation takes time. Trust me, it's worth the wait. You just might be in the process of digging the depth of the hole in which God is about to pour His foundation for you to soar.

Application

1. What might going deep in the foundation of faith look like in your life?
2. How does waiting on God build a deep foundation?
3. What do you think God is building in you while you wait?

Prayer

Father, enable me to go deep with You so that You can build my life into a tall skyscraper. Amen.

THE *WAIT* THAT UNVEILS THE MYSTERY

The eye of the Lᴏʀᴅ is on those who fear Him, on those who wait for His faithfulness.

—PSALM 33:18

After I got cut as a professional football player, I didn't give up on my dream. I wound up playing in the NFL for five years. Throughout my career, everything that *could* go wrong *did* go wrong. The whole time, I felt like God was punishing me. He knew this was the dream I had always wanted, but despite how much I desired it, nothing was working out for me. I kept asking God why He was allowing this to happen when He knew this was all I'd ever dreamed of.

When I retired from the NFL in 2009, I was still asking why and saw myself as a failure. Two years later, the Cowboys called me back—only not to play but to pray!

As I stood in the tunnel for the first game as their chaplain, I realized God was saying, *This was My plan from the very beginning. I knew that your greatest misery would become your greatest ministry. You are now fully prepared to relate to the players in every aspect of their unique lives. This includes your ability to minister to their struggles after enduring your own. I knew My plan was great—that's why I made you wait.*

I finally understood. The location of the Gospel on the field of life was much more important than my location in connection with my personal dreams.

If you're struggling and asking God why, just wait. He's working out your greatest dreams, but it may be in a different way from what you expect.

Application

1. What's something you're currently waiting for God to do for you?
2. What might He be doing in you to prepare you for something greater?
3. Why do you think God's timing is different from ours?

Prayer

God, forgive me for the times I've doubted You and blamed You for my plans not working out. Thank You that Your grace continues to work in me. Amen.

WAITING OUT THE BAD FOR GOOD

> Pray in my behalf, that speech may be given to me in the opening of my mouth, to make known with boldness the mystery of the gospel, for which I am an ambassador in chains; that in proclaiming it I may speak boldly, as I ought to speak.
>
> —EPHESIANS 6:19–20

In 1963 Martin Luther King, Jr., was imprisoned for doing something good—for seeking the welfare and rights of Black Americans nationwide. From 1960 to 1966 John Lewis wound up in prison forty times for the belief that everyone deserved equal treatment and equal access in our country. These people landed in jail for fighting for justice, for doing good. As a result, it gave many more people the courage to advance the ball of justice. And because more people stood up, society had to change. That's how it works.

That's why Paul wasn't complaining in his prison. He was praising God because he knew how God operates. He knew what was more important than his own personal comfort. There were people who needed to hear the Gospel, and Paul was doing his part to get the message to them.

Though you may not be called to wait in a literal prison, at some point while doing good, you will find yourself in some kind of prison. Don't sit in your personal cell in sadness. You may be concerned about what you are going through or where you are in life. But God is trying to prepare you for the great things He has for you up ahead.

Application

1. When have you suffered for doing good?
2. How can you wait well when suffering for doing good?
3. What can you ask God to do for you during this period?

Prayer

God, strengthen and embolden me so that I can continue to speak and do what is right. And so that, like Paul, I can see myself as an ambassador in chains for You. Amen.

WAITING TAKES PATIENCE

Wait for the LORD; be strong and let your heart take courage; yes, wait for the LORD.

—PSALM 27:14

Dallas Cowboys quarterback Dak Prescott experienced deep grief, insomnia, anxiety, and depression from the death of his older brother during the 2020 COVID-19 lockdown. As Dak waited for healing from his grief, he talked openly about his mental health during one of the hardest seasons of his life and shared with the world what he was going through.

Surprisingly his willingness to speak out brought criticism. One high-profile sports newscaster declared that Dak's admission showed a weakness in him. The criticism took the story to a whole new level. As his story trended, more eyes saw Dak's story, and more hearts realized that depression can be walked through.

Millions of struggling people, who were sitting in their own dark rooms at the edge of the cliff, saw their hero saying he understood their feelings of despair. But he also knew that a person can push through to a stronger tomorrow if they don't give up on the grieving and healing process.

Dak's personal imprisonment set many other people free. Don't be afraid to share about the difficulty of the wait—but remember to include the power that comes from it. The progress of God's kingdom is always greater than any difficulties you could ever face. Remember this truth. It'll keep you on life's treadmill when you want to step off. Hang in there. A greater glory waits on the other side of pain.

Application

1. Do you believe God is at work in your waiting season?
2. Do you believe God doesn't waste pain? Why or why not?
3. As you prayerfully consider the pain that so many people in the Bible endured—including Jesus—how can that help you in your current hardship?

Prayer

Father, even when criticism comes my way, let me remain faithfully trusting that You are at work behind the scenes. And I will continue to wait for my healing. Amen.

PART 8

YES, DESPITE THE MOTIVES

> What then? Only that in every way, whether in pretense or in truth, Christ is proclaimed; and in this I rejoice. Yes, and I will rejoice.
>
> —PHILIPPIANS 1:18 NASB1995

Paul learned in prison that some Christians were preaching Christ without a pure heart or pure motives. They preached to get something out of it.

Paul responded in a way that would surprise most of us—and he used one word to get our attention: *yes*.

The word *yes* can be used a lot of ways. It's a word to affirm a question. When he used it, Paul let us know that his next statement wasn't just off the cuff. He'd thought it through.

He said, "*Yes*, and I will rejoice."

He didn't care about their motives; as long as they were proclaiming Christ, he was happy. Paul says this as if he's explaining what he's choosing to do, even though others may object.

Yes, I've made my decision. Yes, I know what I'm doing. Yes, I'm in my right mind. Yes, I am able to do this. Yes, this is an option on the table. Yes, I will have joy even when others are pursuing goals with the wrong motives because they want me out of the way to grab the spotlight. Yes.

I don't know about you, but when I understand Paul's response, I realize that I need to take on that same attitude. As long as Christ is preached, even though others' motives may not be to wish me well, I can still determine to rejoice. Maybe you can too. *Yes.*

Application

1. Do you find it easy or difficult to rejoice when others seem to compete against you to get ahead in their "greatness"?

2. Paul is all about making sure people hear the Gospel, no matter how that happens. Do you think he's right to rejoice?

3. Does his announcement surprise you?

Prayer

God, help me see the bigger issue and to rejoice always when others are sharing the good news of Your love. Amen.

MAKING *YES* A MATTER OF WILL

Rejoice in the Lord always; again I will say, rejoice!
—PHILIPPIANS 4:4

Over the course of two years, I found myself in an emotional and spiritual prison. I lost my cousin, two uncles, my aunt, my grandfather, and my mom all within a short period. Yet while I was struggling to catch my breath under the weight of these compounding waves of grief, I was continuing in a national ministry, writing a book, working at our church, and parenting. I'd been hit with so much, I found myself struggling, and I didn't know how to get through it.

Paul's words helped, even though they seemed odd. Rejoice . . . *always*? As I applied Paul's words in my own situation, I started wondering how Paul was able to still have joy and praise God while in jail. I understood that Paul rejoiced by choice and not because of circumstances. He had made a decision not of his feelings but of his *will*: Rejoice . . . always. Yes, I will say it again . . . rejoice.

Most people are conditional about when they rejoice and even more conditional when it comes to praising God. Most people rejoice and give God praise only when they feel like it or when something good happens. But Paul was behind bars. He was hungry, dirty, uncomfortable, and most likely sleep deprived. And yet he chose to rejoice in spite of his circumstances. Maybe the secret was that he wasn't rejoicing in himself, but in the Lord. If he could do that, then we certainly can too.

Application

1. How often do you rejoice in difficult circumstances?
2. Do you think rejoicing is tied to God's strength and provision in your life?
3. What do you need to do to make rejoicing part of your life in every circumstance?

Prayer

God, I praise and thank You that You are still in control, even when life is difficult, and that You still want to use me. Amen.

THE *YES* OF "IN," NOT "FOR"

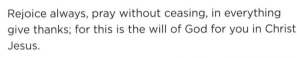

> Rejoice always, pray without ceasing, in everything give thanks; for this is the will of God for you in Christ Jesus.
>
> —1 THESSALONIANS 5:16–18

I knew a couple who were building a house, and one of the construction workers fell from the second floor all the way down to the basement, shattering his leg. When they discovered the construction company had allowed their insurance to lapse, the couple were dumbfounded. When the worker turned around and sued them, they were stunned. They ended up paying out tens of thousands of dollars and were unable to continue with their project. So how are they supposed to rejoice?

Perhaps you've found yourself in the midst of a devastating situation—the medical tests come back positive for cancer, your child gets arrested for drug possession, your spouse betrays you, your parents get divorced. And Paul is directing you to rejoice. Really?

Yes! But he also lets us in on a secret. He didn't say, "Rejoice, yes, give thanks *for* everything"; he said to rejoice *in* everything. There's a difference.

What happens to us may be out of our control, but how we respond to it is always within our control. The couple wasn't thankful that they got sued, but they were thankful that the worker didn't die. The test may come back positive, but we can still be thankful that the doctor caught it. If we say yes to being thankful, then we can find all sorts of reasons to rejoice in all sorts of circumstances.

Application

1. What's the difference between being thankful in circumstances versus being thankful for them? Why is that important?

2. In what difficult situation did you find yourself being grateful? How did that affect your outlook and ability to persevere?

3. How does being thankful in every circumstance make saying yes to God's call easier?

Prayer

Father, I will let my first response be to give You praise in all my circumstances, whether in easy days or difficult times, because I know You are working for my good. Amen.

THE *YES* OF A SHORT-TERM MEMORY

> One thing I do: forgetting what lies behind and reaching forward to what lies ahead, I press on toward the goal for the prize of the upward call of God in Christ Jesus.
>
> —PHILIPPIANS 3:13–14

I love watching football cornerbacks. They amaze me. Essentially, cornerbacks have to guard someone despite having no idea where that someone is going. They have to backpedal when their opponent is running forward. They have to run sideways when the person they're covering is running ahead. They have to constantly observe, assess, adjust, move, chase. That's why coaches often tell their cornerbacks that they need to have a short-term memory—because cornerbacks need to let go of the past and *will* themselves into conquering the next play. If a cornerback doesn't operate with a short-term memory and instead holds on to the fact that he just got beat on the last play, he'll continue to get beat. And it will become a cycle of getting beat.

Paul understood the importance of having a short-term memory. He knew we would never get ahead and claim the victory God has for us if we kept beating ourselves up over our past. So he told us that he practiced short-term memory techniques: "forgetting what lies behind." And in that forgetting, he was able to reach toward the goal. We need to practice short-term memory, forgetting the times we've messed up, so that we too can reach forward to our greatness in Christ.

Application

1. Do you ever beat yourself up over past mistakes or sins?
2. What does "forgetting what lies behind" mean to you?
3. What are some practical ways you can work on forgetting what lies behind you to reach forward in Christ?

Prayer

Lord, sometimes I let my past ruin my present and my future. Give me short-term memory where I need it so that I can reach toward the victorious plans You have for me. Amen.

SAYING *YES* TO JOY VERSUS HAPPINESS

Do not be grieved, for the joy of the LORD is your refuge.

—NEHEMIAH 8:10

Most Americans will tell you that they want to be happy. When I'm counseling or giving advice, I hear people tell me, "Hey, J, I just want to be happy." I smile, because I already know where that story goes. If someone is chasing after happiness, then they are chasing something that was designed to be elusive. See, *happiness* is contingent upon what is *happening*. And because you and I can't control everything that is happening, we cannot catch, hold on to, secure, and maintain happiness. It ebbs and flows as the circumstances ebb and flow. Nobody's circumstances will ever be 100 percent happiness-worthy. Why? Because we live in a sinful world.

Many people today are tired. They are on a constant sprint after happiness. Yet happiness, even when we do catch it, is fleeting. The referee blows his whistle as soon as we make the grab. The play is over. Start again.

So if happiness is based on what is happening, what then is joy? Joy is based on an internal faith. Joy involves trusting God no matter what happens. Joy means believing what God has told us will come about. It involves a heartfelt belief that God's Word is true. Joy isn't fleeting, so when we choose to rejoice, even if the winds and waves crash down on us, we are safe because we connect to the solid rock of Jesus Christ, our strength and refuge.

Application

1. What does it mean that the "joy of the Lord is your refuge"?
2. When have you chased after happiness and discovered it was fleeting?
3. Have you ever felt the joy of the Lord in surprising ways?

Prayer

God, I'm tired of chasing after happiness, thinking it will satisfy, when what I really need is Your deep abiding joy. Help me experience what it really means to have joy in the Lord. Amen.

SAY *YES* TO THE FUNDAMENTALS

> Seek first His kingdom and His righteousness, and all these things will be provided to you.
>
> —MATTHEW 6:33

I've watched a lot of football games, especially high school and college, when a team loses and the announcer says the loss was because the team didn't "stick to the fundamentals." That sounds like a reason some of us fail or have setbacks as we pursue the plans God has for us. Often we don't want to stick to the fundamentals to get us to victory. What are those fundamentals? Grounding our lives in the Word of God, investing in community in a strong church, becoming answerable to another person or accountability group, and spending time with God in prayer. Those are all things we need to say yes to in order to grow in our faith and mature toward a strong future.

God put those fundamentals in place for our success. As J. C. Ryle said, "[The Christian] who seeks first God's kingdom shall never lack anything that is for his good. He may not have so much health as some. He may not have so much wealth as others. He may not have a richly spread table, or royal dainties. But he shall always have *enough.*"* Stick with the fundamentals. Stick with what works, and seek first God's kingdom.

Application

1. Which of the fundamentals do you struggle most to stick to? Why?
2. In what ways does sticking to the fundamentals help us?
3. What practical step or steps can you take today to ensure you stick to the fundamentals?

Prayer

God, I know the importance of sticking to the fundamentals. And I understand why You put them in place. I want to practice them over and over so I can experience real victory in my life and serve You. Amen.

*Rev. J. C. Ryle, *Expository Thoughts on the Gospels: St. Luke*, vol. 2 (New York: Robert Carter & Brothers, 1860), 81.

SAY *YES* TO WHERE YOU ARE HEADED

> To obtain an inheritance which is imperishable, unde-filed, and will not fade away, reserved in heaven for you.
>
> —1 PETER 1:4

My wife, Kanika, and I started homeschooling our kids when the COVID-19 pandemic hit. While Kanika handles the bulk of the teaching, I get to do the fun stuff—the field trips. On one trip, we visited a friend's garden. I wanted the kids to see the plants, the soil, and what it takes for food to grow. Now, my son J2 wasn't feeling it. As we continued, he started to complain and act out.

I took him to the side. "With the way you're acting, you're not going to be able to go swimming in Kelli's pool. I brought everyone's swimsuits, but it looks like you're gonna have to sit this one out because of your attitude."

J2's eyes opened wide. All of a sudden, he began cheer-fully cutting okra and tossing it into the pail like he was taking shots in a basketball game. He was dancing. He was making up songs.

"J2, how are you dancing in the garden now when you were miserable just a minute ago?" I asked.

"It's simple," he said. "You told me that next up is the pool!"

J2 could now dance in his place of misery because he understood where his father was taking him and he changed his focus.

God has a good plan for you and me. In His Word, He has given us a glimpse of where we are going after the hard work of this earth: heaven. So let's change our focus and keep our eyes on the prize!

Application

1. What happens to our mindset when we change our focus from earthly struggles to our heavenly reward?
2. In what areas do you need to change your focus?
3. What step will you take today to make sure you keep your focus on the prize?

Prayer

Focus my eyes on You, Lord, and the vision of Your kingdom. Let that focus keep my mindset on being victorious. Amen.

PART 9

NOW IS YOUR TIME

> Do this, knowing the time, that it is already the hour for you to awaken from sleep; for now salvation is nearer to us than when we first believed.
>
> —ROMANS 13:11

When my siblings and I learned that my mom had been diagnosed with stage 4 terminal cancer, we didn't know how to take it. We felt beaten, bruised.

"I understand that you are sad," Mom said. "I have every expectation that you will love me, care for me, pray for me, and be there for me. But God has an expectation too. And that is that you always remember, through thick and thin, that you are here to serve His purposes. That's the reason you exist. And everything—including pain and anguish, even what seems counterintuitive, even what you didn't expect—is all a distraction to keep you from the reason you are here. So stand up, hold your head up, and be strong. Continue to do the work of the ministry."

We let my mom's words sink in as she continued, "If you are called to preach, you will preach. If you are called to write, you will write. If you are called to proclaim, you will proclaim. If you are called to lead a Bible study, you will lead it."

She was right. You and I are on a journey, and as we set out to embrace what God has given us, we will face opposition. We will face unexpected lows. But no matter what we face, we must remember this: We are here to serve the purposes of God—and the time to do that is right *now*.

Application

1. What distractions are keeping you from serving the purposes of God?
2. In what ways can you refocus to get back to your main purpose on this earth?
3. What is God calling you to do right now?

Prayer

God, with determination may I see distractions for what they are—those things that attempt to keep me from serving You and from what You have in store for me. Amen.

TAKING YOUR PROMISED LAND *NOW*

Joshua said to the people, "Consecrate yourselves,
for tomorrow the LORD will do miracles among you."

—JOSHUA 3:5

The Israelites had arrived at the Promised Land. The only thing that stood between them and it was the Jordan River, which they were going to cross with the Lord's miraculous help—just as He had helped them cross the Red Sea many years before. So Joshua, Israel's leader, told the people to get ready, to consecrate themselves, so they would be acceptable for God's purposes for them.

God is telling you to do the same. You are so close. Your promised land is just over the horizon. Do not stop. Do not drop your head. Do not slow down because obstacles are in your path. Keep moving forward. How? By keeping focused on how you think, speak, and act. You are not waiting on your time to arrive. Your time is *now*. But Satan will try to convince you otherwise. He will try to distract you.

Stay true to God and obey Him in all things. Be bold as you move forward—because God is *for* you! You don't have to wait for everything to be perfect and all the conditions to be right before you serve God. You serve Him right now, right where you are, with what you have at your disposal.

Application

1. Why did Joshua call the people to consecrate themselves to accept God's miracles?
2. What does consecrating yourself mean?
3. In what ways can you prepare for the miracles God is getting ready to do in your life?

Prayer

Lord, thank You that You have faithfully brought me to the promised land. I don't need to wait to grab hold of what You have planned for me. I can push forward now and receive it. Thank You, Lord! Amen.

LIVING *NOW* FOR A GOOD PLAYBACK

> We must all appear before the judgment seat of Christ, so that each one may receive compensation for his deeds done through the body, in accordance with what he has done, whether good or bad.
>
> —2 CORINTHIANS 5:10

What do you think every football player is thinking about during their game? They're thinking about the next day. Why? Because that's when they review the film and account for their previous performance, whether good or not.

On review day, our coach would pull down the screen, turn on the overhead projector, pick up the red pointer, and ask, "Were you out there bearing the image of the uniform that I gave you, based on the playbook I wrote for you to execute? Or were you out there doing your own thing? Playing your own game? We're about to watch the film right now."

The same is true of us. We cannot lose focus, no matter what we face, because our mission is to pursue this thing called life with tomorrow in mind. Our focus must be on Christ, not the crisis. On God, not the grind. On obedience, not the obstacles. Because one day God is going to pull down His cosmic screen, turn on His spiritual overhead projector, and pick up His red blood-of-Jesus pointer. And His only concern will be this: "Did you serve my purposes? Or did you play by your own schemes? We're going to watch the film right now."

Since God gave us this life, He will certainly also give us all we need to live it well. So it's time now to pursue that life.

Application

1. Are you living with "tomorrow's" playback film in mind?
2. If you were to face God now, what would your life's film look like?
3. What steps can you take today to ensure your playback looks strong?

Prayer

Lord, empower me to live well so that when it's time to play back the film footage of my life, You will say of me, "Well done, My good and faithful servant." Amen.

GOD HAS QUALIFIED YOU *NOW*

By faith the prostitute Rahab, because she welcomed the spies, was not killed with those who were disobedient.

—HEBREWS 11:31 NIV

When the Israelite spies went to Jericho, Rahab—a prostitute—hid them to keep them safe from the people in that city who refused to obey God. Rahab didn't consider her past or even her present flaws. She simply allowed God to use her.

God doesn't always call the qualified. But He always qualifies the called. He specializes in using flawed people who believe in Him. These people believe that their present weaknesses and past failures can be overcome, even used to their advantage, because they say yes to God working in their lives.

We don't need to be chasing comments, chasing views, chasing notoriety when God has already commented, viewed, and given notice of His purpose for us. Getting what God has given us is easier than we often make it out to be. It's all about abiding in Him and letting Him work out His goals both in and through us.

Align your heart with Christ's, and He will reveal to you His will, His plan, His purpose for your life right now, and His strength for you to carry it out.

Application

1. What flaws in your past or present are keeping you from pursuing God's greatness in your life?
2. How does Rahab's story change the way you see how God uses unqualified people?
3. How does it make you feel to realize that God doesn't hold you back from His purposes because you aren't "qualified"?

Prayer

Lord, I am flawed and unqualified. But thank You that You qualify the unqualified. Thank You that You redeem the flaws so that I can experience the greatness You have in store for me. Let me reach for that greatness now and always. Amen.

NOW IS THE TIME TO STOP CHASING THE WRONG THINGS

Blessed are those whose way is blameless, who walk in the Law of the Lᴏʀᴅ. Blessed are those who comply with His testimonies, and seek Him with all their heart.

—PSALM 119:1–2

Growing up, I had a toy poodle named Solomon. He loved to run around in circles, chasing his own tail. I'd get home from school and see this dog pursuing his tail, and I would think, *Does this dog not know that his mouth is on his face and his tail is on his rear end? He wasn't created to catch his own tail. That's just a lot of movement with no progress.*

One day Solomon finally caught his own tail! He held on to it until he apparently realized how futile it was, and then he finally let it go, because he was too uncomfortable to stay in that position.

I imagine he had a moment of dog satisfaction when he eventually caught what he had been chasing for so long. But he couldn't stay like that!

Sometimes we can get so involved in what we are doing that we are not actually progressing. We're just running in circles. We're chasing something that will never satisfy and could never last even if we did eventually catch it. We are setting our own target with our own tails. Which is why we can spend a lifetime chasing after something only to find out, at the end, that it was the wrong something all along.

To get what God has given you right now, regain your focus and put it where it needs to be—on the Gospel of Jesus Christ and the advancement of His kingdom.

Application

1. In what ways do Christians often chase their own tails?
2. Have you ever felt like you were chasing your own tail? Why?
3. What made you stop?

Prayer

God, whenever I am tempted to chase my tail, remind me of what I'm chasing so I can refocus on what really matters. Amen.

THE URGENCY OF PRESSING ON *NOW*

> Blessed is a man who perseveres under trial; for once he has been approved, he will receive the crown of life which the Lord has promised to those who love Him.
>
> —JAMES 1:12

A few years ago, I lost my dear friend and cousin Wynter Pitts at the age of thirty-eight. Her heart just stopped. Not long after that, my cousin Michael, who was only twenty-eight, lost his wife, who was just thirty. She found out that she had a tumor and passed away the very next day. My grandfather, Two-Daddy and the original Kingdom Man as we called him, died just a month before my mom passed away.

The pain is real—I deeply understand. And though we grieve whatever our loss—whether the loss of someone close to us, the loss of dreams, the loss of a business, the loss of health, the loss of income, or the loss of relational harmony—we must press on. Evil doesn't give us a break just because we grieve. That's exactly the time we can get hit the hardest—when we're already down. So we must prepare ourselves to go on the offensive in this thing called life. We press on no matter what our circumstances, for it is our perseverance, as James tells us, that matures and approves us to receive the crown of life. There are no time-outs, no time to wait. It's urgent for us to keep pressing on.

Application

1. Do you find it difficult to persevere in the midst of loss?
2. Why is it important for us to persevere when we're down?
3. In what way does perseverance mature us and make us approved in God's kingdom?

Prayer

Father, pressing on during the easy times is easy, but those times aren't what mature us, I know. Help me to stay faithful to You when I face loss. Remind me that You are always faithful and trustworthy to me even when I don't understand life's losses. Amen.

NOW HELP EMPOWER OTHERS TO SUCCEED

> Jonathan, Saul's son, set out and went to David at Horesh, and encouraged him in God.
>
> —1 SAMUEL 23:16

Jonathan and David were close friends. And God used Jonathan in a special way in David's life. David had been anointed and established to be Israel's next king, which didn't sit too well with the current king, Saul. So angered by this news, Saul put David on his hit list. One day when King Saul was searching for David to take his life, Jonathan set out to find his friend, and then he helped David find strength in God—he encouraged and lifted him up. Jonathan acted as a life builder, and God used him to develop David to spiritual maturity.

We have been called to greatness, and part of that greatness is to help others spiritually mature. That means we pray unceasingly for them (1 Samuel 12:23), rejoice and weep with them (Romans 12:15), bear their burdens (Galatians 6:2), and encourage them (1 Thessalonians 5:11).

Being victorious in God's kingdom isn't an individual pursuit. We need others, just as they need us, to keep going, to never grow weary, to hold each other accountable. It's the Golden Rule—treating people the same way we want them to treat us (Matthew 7:12). This is the way we please God.

Application

1. Think of a time when you needed encouragement and someone lifted your spirit and motivated you to keep pressing on. What did that person say or do?
2. When people think of you, do they think of someone who is willing to encourage and help them along the way?
3. Consider how often you say, "Well done!" to others—whether to your family, to your friends, at work, or at church. How can you more intentionally build others up in their faith?

Prayer

God, since You also place others in our path to encourage us and build us toward spiritual maturity, let me always be available and willing to be that encourager to others in their pursuit of Your kingdom. Amen.

THE *NOW* OF LIVING BETWEEN HEAVEN AND EARTH

> I have fought the good fight, I have finished the course, I have kept the faith; in the future there is reserved for me the crown of righteousness, which the Lord, the righteous Judge, will award to me on that day.
>
> —2 TIMOTHY 4:7–8

December 30, 2019, was the last day I spent time with my mom. A week before that, she was living between heaven and earth. She would say things like, "Do you see my mom? She was just sitting over there." Or Mom would ask, "Do you see these colors? They are unbelievable. So beautiful!" We would smile because Mom was seeing what we could not.

But one thing she said stayed with me: "The award! They are about to give me my award!"

When I heard her make this announcement, I felt peace. "Enjoy that award, Mom," I said.

Through thick and thin, she served. Whether receiving no attention or a lot of attention, she served. In times of little money and in times of having enough, she served.

In seasons of health and in seasons of sickness, she served the purposes of God. Right through to the finish.

The truth is that there is a reward for those who keep fighting, who finish the course, who keep the faith. There is a reward for all you do for Christ. So don't lose your focus. Keep striving. Keep pursuing. You will get all that God has planned for you both in time and in eternity when you choose to serve His purposes. And *now* is as good a time as any to keep moving—*your* time is now!

Application

1. What does it mean to fight the good fight of faith?
2. What is the most difficult thing you've ever accomplished? What was it like to finish?
3. How can you finish the race well in this life?

Prayer

Father, help me to fight faithfully so I can finish the course and receive my reward. Thank You, Lord! Amen.

ABOUT
THE AUTHOR

Jonathan Evans is a pastor, speaker, mentor, and author who speaks passionately and powerfully about his relationship with God and has a burning desire to share his faith with others. He serves on the pastoral staff at Oak Cliff Bible Fellowship, a nondenominational church in Dallas, Texas, with his pastor, friend, and father, Dr. Tony Evans. Jonathan has roles in both the local church and in the national ministry, the Urban Alternative.

Jonathan has a goal of building a legacy that leaves an impact. A dynamic speaker, he has shared at men's conferences, youth events, churches, and other venues throughout the United States. Jonathan has also written several books, including *Different*, *Get in the Game: A Spiritual Workout for Athletes* (with Dr. Tony Evans), and *Kingdom Family Devotional* (with Dr. Tony Evans). Jonathan has also created powerful video and audio presentations to accompany his teaching, including spoken-word videos that showcase his ability to deliver his messages with energy, creativity, and relevance.

Before serving as a pastor, Jonathan was an NFL fullback for the Dallas Cowboys after playing college football at Baylor University and a season with the Berlin Thunder of the European NFL. During his career he also was on the roster of the San Diego Chargers, Tennessee Titans, Buffalo Bills, Washington Redskins, and Houston Texans. He currently serves as the chaplain for the Dallas Cowboys.

In addition, Jonathan is the founder of Generate Nation, an outreach of Oak Cliff Bible Fellowship and a ministry that focuses on young adults.

More from Jonathan Evans

God has a purpose for you *right now.* As you read about the Old Testament leader Joshua as a model for stepping up to God's big calling, you will be inspired to discover how God wants to use you in His kingdom. If you will be steadfast and always abound in God's calling, you'll see that it will not be in vain. God wants to do great things through you!

Your Time Is Now